Women's Writings from India, Pakistan and Bangladesh

Women's Writings from India, Pakistan and Bangladesh

The Worlds of *Bangla* and *Urdu*

Edited by

Rakhshanda Jalil
Debjani Sengupta

BLOOMSBURY
NEW DELHI • LONDON • OXFORD • NEW YORK • SYDNEY

BLOOMSBURY INDIA
Bloomsbury Publishing India Pvt. Ltd
Second Floor, LSC Building No. 4, DDA Complex, Pocket C – 6 & 7
Vasant Kunj, New Delhi 110070

BLOOMSBURY, BLOOMSBURY INDIA and the Diana logo
are trademarks of Bloomsbury Publishing Plc

First published in India 2019
This edition published 2019

ISBN: HB: 978-93-88271-52-3; eBook: 978-93-88271-54-7

2 4 6 8 10 9 7 5 3 1

Typeset by Manipal Digital
Printed and bound in India

CONTENTS

Acknowledgements

This volume of contemporary women's writings in Bangla from the subcontinent owes a great debt of gratitude to all the authors who have generously permitted me to use their works. I take great pleasure to acknowledge my debt to their camaraderie and good humour, especially when I pestered them for any help during the processes of translation. I am deeply grateful to Joyadi (Joya Mitra), Apa (Selina Hossain), Sunanda Bhattacharya, Kalyani Thakur, Manju Bala, Sujata Roy, Papree Rahman, Anita Agnihotri, Jhumur Pandey and Maitry Roy Moulik for being such extraordinary wordsmiths who have laid bare in words their incredibly political engagements with our contemporary realities. Their writings resonate with a passionate engagement with issues of equality, rights and justice that deeply move readers. I am, therefore, very humbled to have been entrusted with translating their works, and I hope the pieces collected here will find a safe harbour in the minds and hearts of our gentle readers! This book owes a great debt to Rakhshanda Jalil, my co-editor, who supported and cajoled me to come on board for the project. A special thanks goes to Chandra Sekhar of Bloomsbury who believed in this book. Thanks to Shreya Chakraborti and Arnab Karmakar for their meticulous editing interventions. I am grateful to Sandipan Sen, Kaisar Haq, Niaz Zaman and Rani Ray for their help and support. My deepest thanks to Shahruk Rahman, Rajorshi Das, Lipika Das and Saheli Biswas for agreeing to translate three difficult stories.

I am especially indebted to Valsala Kuriakose and Kuriakose Mamkoottam, Carmela and Miguel Coquis, and

Franziska Krisch—this book is a small recompense for their abiding affections and sustained generosities.

Debjani Sengupta
Delhi, July 2019

I echo Debjani's words in recording my gratitude to all the contributors of this volume: the authors themselves, their translators and, most importantly, those who suggested authors whose works I should read and include here. Among the latter, I must gratefully acknowledge Asif Aslam Farrukhi, his generosity and kindness in not just suggesting authors and titles but also helping me locate them, especially the works of Pakistani writers that are not easily available on our side of the border. And it is to Asif that I dedicate this selection of Urdu writings from South Asia.

I am grateful to Daisy Rockwell, fellow traveller on the sometimes rocky, sometimes smooth road to translations, for her immaculate translation of Aniqa Naz's unusual story *Roll of the Dice* as well as Azra Abbas's *Fragrance*.

A special thanks to Chandra Sekhar of Bloomsbury, and to Debjani, my co-editor, with memories of times well spent discussing what should and should not go in this collection of writings.

Rakhshanda Jalil
Delhi, July 2019

Introduction

This book is the product of a moment of epiphany. In the summer of 2018, as the two of us sat talking about contemporary literary genres from the subcontinent, it occurred to us that a volume of writings from Bangla and Urdu might be a good way to raise issues of language, identity, nationhood and aspects of feminism and women's writing in the subcontinent. Earlier, we had worked as translators together with two different languages, Urdu and Bangla, and we had felt that there were peculiar resonances in the history of these languages that were obvious but significant. Both these languages have lived a life across political borders and are spoken, read and loved by people across diverse geographical sites including a large diaspora. Both languages have had an afterlife after 1947 that helped them to refashion their cultural spheres in a divided land. Therefore, it can be claimed even by the most indifferent of practitioners that the linguistic and cultural dimensions of Urdu and Bangla continue to be vibrant, diverse, and meaningful in ways that are sometimes overwhelming to map and ascertain. It dawned on us that as translators and editors, we are happily placed in a situation where we can bring these languages together, side by side in a book, to perhaps speak to each other and to showcase their strengths. By creating a platform for contemporary literary works, especially by women, we felt we would get a new, radical view of the ways in which these languages have shaped women's creative universes.

The linguistic trajectories of Urdu and Bangla before and after 1947 are well known so we have nothing more to add to that. However, it also felt strange to us that given this mirror semblance of their past histories across political and physical borders, few have thought to bring them together before. Urdu's presence in Pakistan and Bangla's in Bangladesh have obvious resonances in India as well, so there is a commonality and shared history that we can neither ignore nor be indifferent to. Have our internecine fratricides overshadowed our relationships in the linguistic spheres as well? This is a question that no one can clearly answer at this juncture but given this shared world in the subcontinent that we inhabit, we thought the time was ripe to create a volume that would physically bring the two languages together. We thought it would be our own way to show ourselves and to our readers that there were more things that united people in the subcontinent than that divided them. We are, of course, aware of the limitations of anthologies in that, and the motives behind their creations are never simple and clear-cut. Editors bring on board their own ideas and prejudices about issues concerning language and representations. When the volume brings together translations with their own inherent politics, the motives become even more complex. However, in any anthology, the fundamental principle ought to be the gathering together, as in a bouquet, of the myriad voices of diverse authors so that they speak to each other in subtle and complex ways. Of course, there is an element of luck in all this. The search for new writers and texts can face many obstacles of access and permission, but we have been incredibly lucky in our venture. We have collected in these pages a formidable array of voices that we are sure will add new, critical dimensions to writings by women in the subcontinent.

Urdu Section

An unknown fear
Was imbued in her
From the day she was born
—Zehra Nigah, in 'Dildar Begum is Buried Here'

The tradition of *ecriture feminine* ('writing the feminine') is not a very old one in Urdu and in prose, especially fiction—it is just about a 100-odd-year old. There have always been men writing as women, that is, *in* women's voices or *of* women and *about* women, making women both the subject and the predicate. It took a long time for women to find a real voice in Urdu literature. In Urdu poetry, while the voice may be that of a lovelorn woman suffering from the pangs of separation, a discontented concubine, or a young woman on the verge of marriage, the writer was invariably a man. And it has been regarded as perfectly acceptable for men to write in women's voices on so-called women's issues expressing womanly concerns. This vocal masquerade has been taking place for centuries and has been taken quite for granted.

Chand Bibi (1768–1820), better known as Mah Laqa Bai Chanda, is popularly believed to be the first published woman poet in Urdu. A courtesan dancer in the princely state of Hyderabad, she moved from seducing men for money and power to pursuing a mystical devotion to Maula Ali—a movement that is amply reflected in her poetic oeuvre. Displaying an extraordinary blend of Shia piety (almost all her poems contain an invocation to Maula Ali) and seductive power, she is at once elegant, articulate and yet unconventional. An example of her literary prowess is as follows:

I'll toss the record of Chanda's deeds into
passion's churning waves
If Ali, the forgiver of my sins, with
a wine-cup my way comes.

And,

Oh Ali, keep Chanda glowing with a
ray of your brilliance
As the sun is illuminated each day as
your radiance pours out.

Being a woman is central to her poetry, even though she occasionally adopts the gendered voice of a man pursuing a beloved; even these seemingly masculine poems end with her returning to a female persona in the closing line of the ghazal as 'Ali's servant-girl'. Mah Laqa's poetry seems to constantly challenge the accepted notion of a woman's place in society, that too, a society governed by a largely Islamic worldview. She was a woman, a poet, a dancer and a singer who also used to advise the Nizam and his ministers in political matters. She was a patron of the arts too, who kept and schooled young women in music and dance and encouraged poets, calligraphers and painters. In no way typical of her time, her city, her religious community or even her profession, she manipulated her femininity and her legendary beauty to achieve her artistic and spiritual goals.

After Mah Laqa Bai, there was a long gap when women from '*shareef*' families would either not write poetry, or not write it for public consumption. The Mughal harem did indeed have many educated, accomplished, articulate women, some of whom wrote family histories such as Gulbadan Begum, or Sufi treatises, such as Aurangzeb's sister Jahanara. But it was left to the historian to excavate these 'lost' voices; in their own time and age, they remained cloistered within the *zenana*. For all practical purposes, it has been a long journey from a Mah Laqa Bai to a modern-day woman poet, such as Zehra Nigah.

Zehra Nigah appeared on the literary horizon as a child prodigy in the 1950s and has consistently been hailed as the one voice worth listening to in the babel of the mushaira circuit. When she began to make a mark as a poet in the 1950s and the 1960s, women who recited their poetry in public were a rarity. Women from respectable families were not encouraged to come on stage to recite their poetry, let alone express themselves with any degree of sensuousness. Hence, a young Zehra Nigah hid her femininity behind demureness, read her poems with eyes downcast and scuttled back to the safe haven of domesticity. But the sheer lyricism of her words, the engaging simplicity of her poetic idiom and the sharp insightful comments couched therein built a formidable reputation and amassed a legion of admirers. To this day, a hush invariably descends at noisome mushairas when she stands up to recite her poetry.

Being the senior-most among the Urdu poets chosen here, Zehra Nigah allows us an entry into a discussion on the poets chosen for this volume. Is she a writer of feminine poetry or a feminist poet? She says she views the world around her through the eyes of a woman, yes, but her concerns are not those of a woman alone. She speaks in a woman's tongue, using feminine imagery and idiom to make powerful social and political comments. She has alluded to the bitter fratricidal war that culminated in the creation of Bangladesh as well as the heart-rending situation in Afghanistan. She has written of the repressive Hudood Ordinances introduced during General Zia's oppressive regime in Pakistan as also about love, friendship and small everyday joys and sorrows. In 'Dildar Begum is Buried Here' (*Yahan Dildar Begum Dafan Hain*), she makes a searing indictment of the practice of seclusion and the effect it has on the psyche of the girl child.

Zehra Nigah's younger contemporary, Fahmida Riaz, was a woman of many parts: poet, writer, translator, activist, travel-writer and fearless critic of her country's military dictatorship. While several of her poems, such as 'The Veil and the Four Walls' (*Chaadar aur Char-Diwari*), riled the political and religious establishments, collections like 'The Torn Body' (*Badan Dareeda)* created a furor because of its uninhibited exploration of female sexuality. In 'Aqlima', she brings attention to the lesser-known sibling of Cane and Abel, and the daughter of Adam and Eve. According to Genesis (4:6-16), God spoke to Cain; Fahmida Riyaz is asking: what if He were to have spoken to Aqlima too?

Kishwar Naheed, a formidable voice among contemporary Urdu feminist poets, author of the iconic poem 'We Sinful Women' (*Hum Gunahgar Auratein*) has been a life-long campaigner for women's rights. In 'Wish' (*Khwahish*), she wants to write her own epitaph much like the Urdu short story writer Saadat Hasan Manto, who wrote his own impudent epitaph shortly before his death: 'Here [Manto] lies buried—and buried in his breast are all the secrets of the art of storytelling. Even now weighed down by mounds of earth, he is wondering if he is the greater storyteller or God!' Immodest, yes, but by no means outrageous, for it was true that whatever the merits of Manto's style and craft, he had the rare gift of being able to narrate the most blood-curdling events with faithful accuracy and an unsparing eye for detail. And so, too, with Kishwar Naheed. Her poetry has been a seismograph recording every flutter in the turbulent sociopolitical landscape of her country. And she has reveled in her role as the enfant terrible of Urdu poetry: defiant, outspoken, eminently self-aware and acutely political, she has always delighted in cocking a snook at the Establishment—both literary and otherwise. A former civil servant and editor of a prestigious monthly magazine in Pakistan, she has written extensively on women's issues, crimes against women and the images of women in media and textbooks.

Sara Shagufta, a poet who died tragically young, has become something of an urban legend for her short but turbulent life marked by tragedy and abuse, as well as her remarkable poetry that subverts all the conventions of modern Urdu poetry. Coming in the second wave of feminist poets in Pakistan, after Fahmida Riaz and Kishwar Naheed, she uses poetry as agency, as a means of speaking up when all other avenues are closed to her. She mines her own life and her lived experiences in poems, such as 'Debt' (*Qarz*), to write intensely personal poetry that rises above its time and circumstance and continues to speak to us.

Tarannum Riyaz is an Indian novelist, poet and columnist from Kashmir. In 'Coffins' (*Janaazey*), she speaks of the 'coffin' of domesticity that buries women alive inside their homes and the many, many 'deaths' that women die every day in order to stay alive. Zahida Zaidi's poem too is a portrayal of domesticity marked by its little joys and many sorrows. 'The Crystal Vase' (*Billor ka Jaam*) becomes a metaphor for the intransience of life and beauty for once the vase breaks, the pricking of the shards 'will be felt/In every nerve and fibre...all your life'.

Coming now to the short fiction chosen in this volume, there's Zakia Mashhadi, somewhat of a late-bloomer as a writer. Wrapped in the constraints of domesticity for far too long, she is now well into her seventies, finding her voice and writing robust stories on a host of issues—communalism, sectarianism and yes, gender. Often the translator of her own stories, in 'Man' (*Mard*), she weaves a densely lush tapestry alive with the sound and colour of rural India; a hamlet in the Himalayan foothills is plagued by animal attacks: serpents, leopards, elephants and finally the most bestial of all, Man.

Demonstrating not just the pan-Indian reach of Urdu but also showing us how its use cuts across socio-economic lines and how, increasingly, the Urdu writer is willing to embrace a host of concerns, Sadiqa Nawab Sahar, also, takes us to a provincial town in Maharashtra where a college teacher encounters a poor couple with a sick child. In its seeming guilelessness, 'The Seventh-Month Baby' (*Satwansa*) contains a powerful statement on the limits of bourgeois sympathy for the less fortunate, and the ways in which women fall back on the controls set by their husband and, sometimes, even 'use' those controls to explain or excuse their own shortcomings.

The only two stories from Pakistan here, 'Roll of the Dice' (*Chausar ka Paansa*) by Aniqa Naz and 'Fragrance' (*Khushbu*) by Azra Abbas, in some ways illustrate our understanding of women's writings: that it need not be about solely 'women's issues' and that it need neither be rabidly against patriarchy or vehemently feminist. Our intention in putting this collection of women's writings was as much to showcase precisely what concerns women writers as to demonstrate the range of those concerns; it would seem the world with all its frailties and inconsistencies, as also its elusiveness and subtleties, is—and should be—of interest to a woman writer.

The Urdu of young Aniqa Naz (who died in a car accident) is inflected with the tone and tenor of Karachi; the city's street idiom and nonchalance are amply reflected in this story of casual violence and easy money. With his accomplices 'Tarzan' and 'Virus', the protagonist of this story is a hold-up artist who robs women in buses at gunpoint; his spoken Urdu and his frame of reference is, naturally, different from, say Zakia Mashhadi's story located in the Terai or even Azra Abbas's story whose exact location is unknown but one that speaks of the mystique of a fragrance, a fragrance that has beckoned little girls from across an unknown threshold.

The last of the Urdu stories is 'Draupadi Has Woken Up' (*Draupadi Jaag Utthi*) by Renu Bahl from the Indian side of the Punjab. Her Urdu is inflected with a Punjabiyat that is common to the two Punjabs now divided by an international border. It is also redolent of the countryside and the mores of an agrarian society that, once embarked upon the path of selective pregnancies through sex determination tests, must face the terrible consequences where women become both victims and perpetuators of gender-based discrimination.

Bangla Section

What I intend to write
But never ever can
Those are my true poems
—Mandakranta Sen, *Truth*

In the last decade or two, anthologies of women's writings have been plentiful and diverse in the subcontinent. One recollects the excitement and wonder of the publication of Susie Tharu and K. Lalita's *Women Writing in India* in the 1990s that brought together texts from the 600th BC to the 20th century in two volumes. From then on, as Women's Studies departments took off and consolidated in universities across the country, political, social and economic upheavals in the lives of women in the subcontinent have been reflected in literary writings. These have been brought together and published at different times either through the efforts of the writers themselves or through conscientious editors. Lakshmi Holmström's *The Inner Courtyard: Stories by Indian Women* came out at the same time as Tharu's volumes and other excellent anthologies followed that showcased brilliant authors across the spectrum of Indian languages including those in English translations. Indian publishing industry took a timely stock of the excellent translations from different languages and proactively took out lists of impressive volumes of original works by women or their renderings, including those across the borders. This created an ambient ecosystem for women writers, formidable in their craftsmanship as well as in their political and social awareness. The rise of social media too had provided a necessary platform to newer genres. Therefore, this is an exciting time to think of how our contemporary literary scene is playing out particularly for the women writers of the subcontinent.

Bangla is the state language of Bangladesh and is an official language in West Bengal. It is spoken and written in Tripura and a variation of it can be heard in parts of Assam like in the erstwhile Cachar and Sylhet regions. Bangla has many nuances and dialects, spoken and written, depending on its geographical positioning so the language prevalent in the border areas of West Bengal is markedly different from the Bangla spoken in urban areas like Kolkata. Although in an English translation such variations are difficult to maintain and reinstate, the very fact that these stories are situated in differing regions give them an underlying vitality that represents the varied realities of women living, working and loving in diverse spaces, both marginal and mainstream. The stories and poems that have been collected in the Bangla section have no one common theme in terms of subject matter or style but each of the pieces are written by authors (barring a few) who have never been translated into English or are not so well known in terms of metropolitan publishing practices. However, every one of these writers have one thing in common: their words are deeply political in that they engage with the realities of our existences, especially the inequalities that women continue to face through caste, class and gender relations. In all the pieces collected here, we find not a strident but an inflexible voice that seeks equality, dignity and respect for women's labour, her variegated experiences, her sexuality and her ability to make sense of the world. These writers are extraordinary wordsmiths whose short stories and poems open up a rich and nuanced exploration of the social, economic and political injustices faced by women and men in the subcontinent. From Bangladesh, the works of two wonderful writers are represented in the volume. Selina Hossain's 'The Forestland' (*Bonobhumi*) is a look at the Chakma people's repression in the hands of Bangladeshi army in the Chittagong hill areas. This story is significant in its honest appraisal of the expediencies of state formations in the subcontinent. Papree Rahman's story is a similar tale of marginality (with surreal touches) faced by the urban poor in Dhaka. From West Bengal, we have Joya Mitra's brilliant story 'Sun and a White Bird' (*Surjyo O Shada Pakhiti*) on women Naxal prisoners that articulates a continuity of pain and hope even in peaceful times. Anita Agnihotri's superbly crafted poem 'The Cotton Farmer's Wife' (*Tulo Chashir Bou*) describes the conditions of the victims of the agrarian crisis in present day India. Maitri Roy Moulik is a writer whose short story 'Straw and Chaff' (*Khorkuto*) breaks new grounds in the powerful depiction of women who live in border areas and who do menial work in cities to make ends meet. Sujata Roy's poem 'The Machete' (*Daa*) is about exile and memory in the context of Bengal's Partition in 1947 through the optics of a man's relationship to his land. Manju Bala's poem 'Cannot Stoop Lower' (*Aar Nichey Nambo Naa*) exposes the perpetuation of insidious caste hierarchies in anonymous urban lives and Kalyani Thakur's 'Writing' (*Lekhoni*) is a brilliant short piece on the resistance forged through the ubiquitous pen of the lower caste. From Tripura, we have Sunanda Bhattacharya's moving story *Bandhni* set on the 2002 Gujarat riots and a single woman's search for justice, while from Assam's Barak Valley, we have Jhumur Pandey's lyrical story 'Bonodurga Slakes Her Thirst' (*Jol Khaben Bonodurga*) that features a tea garden worker and her lonely, marginal life.

This section in Bangla comprises ten pieces—stories and poems. While choosing and translating some of them, I was constantly aware of the quiet rage of the texts, their terrible beauty as well as their power to heal. In bringing together this bouquet of brilliant writers, I wish to underline my own personal debt to a language that has shaped my individual history and has influenced the political trajectory of the subcontinent. In that very relationship of the personal and the political, this section takes a much beaten path but hopes to find new resonances in the minds of its gentle readers.

Of course, anthologies are conceived in a certain way, but their afterlife is altogether another matter. We hope that our efforts are not in vain and our readers catch a glimpse of the dynamic and intriguing worlds of the two languages that are alive in these pages. Happy reading!

Rakhshanda Jalil
Debjani Sengupta
Delhi, 2019

Poetry

Dildar Begum is Buried Here

Zehra Nigah

An unknown fear
Was imbued in her
From the day she was born
The fear of a dark chamber
Was steeped in every pore
The terror of falling from a height
Had been dogging every footstep
The habit of hiding behind the lee of a door
Had been her earliest wish
To watch the spectacle in the streets from behind shuttered windows
Had been the first aspiration of her life
As time passed
And the skeins of her brain awakened her body
The spectre of safekeeping grew so terrifying
That she became ashamed of her body
Soon, a little curiosity fluttered through the world of buyers
The sound of a beating heart was muffled
Adorned with the ornaments of fear
Weighed under the countless flowers of hesitancy
The buyers imprisoned her once again into a dark chamber
The same chamber that had terrified her since her childhood
Some semblance of awareness came
As youth passed and the curtains before her eyes parted
To reveal the spectacle of the world
Her feet moved towards the threshold

She had barely set one foot forward when tiny hands appeared, like manacles
Now she stands on a road that is said to be the path of death
The spectacles of the world do not stay fixed in her glazed eyes
Now her feet do not move towards any threshold
The tiny hands have become so big
That they have long since left her palms
Now she is a captive of her own chains
Her dark chamber carries the following inscription:
'Dildar Begum is buried here.
That pure, pious, patient and praise-giving woman sleeps here
Strange men are forbidden to come close by
Those who wish to offer prayers
May do so from a distance.'

Translated from Urdu by Rakhshanda Jalil

Aqlima[1]

Fahmida Riaz

Aqlima
Born of the same mother as Cain and Abel
Of the same mother
But different
Different between her thighs
And in the fullness of her breasts
And inside her belly
In her womb
Why is the sacrifice of a plump sheep
Their only destiny?[2]
A prisoner of her body
She is standing on a burning mount
Under the blistering sun
As though engraved in stone
Look closely at that engraving
Above the long thighs
Above the full breasts
Above the complicated womb
Aqlima has a head too
If only Allah were to address[3] Aqlima some day
And ask her something

Translated from Urdu by Rakhshanda Jalil

---

1 The lesser-known sibling of Cain and Abel
2 One sheep is offered as sacrifice at the time of *aqiqa*, the naming ceremony, in the case of an infant girl in contrast to two for a boy
3 According to Genesis 4:6–16, God spoke to Cain

The Cotton Farmer's Wife

Anita Agnihotri

Why did I leave for my parents' home
Last winter! Oh Death!
The green pea fronds were out,
So were the radish and spinach,
Mother had tied them in a bundle, for me.
That was a chance
For my man and he took it.
And from the beams, not with any rope lying around—
But my blue sari that he had bought,
Twisted in a knot…
Our little girl was in the bed.
He had shoved her out
From the hut…
That silly girl—she went—And—

Whenever I lie down, my eyes
Go up to the beams.
His smiling face, my man swinging—
He saved himself by dying—
A debt of four lakhs and interest too,
He never would have paid back.
There was no rain, the upright crop had burnt,
The black soil had sucked the sweat, pain, drops of blood,
The black soil did not give anything back.

The penalty was pardoned though the subsidy never came—
As time dragged on, the noose had tightened,

The bank agents swore, threatened.
I could not bear it any more, my Wife,
I was afraid the men would drag me through the
neighbourhood, humiliated beyond belief.

You could not bear it but I am mutilated by too many
wounds.
You could leave the world, but I cannot,
For the one in my belly, the one on my lap,
And the other barely six.
The well runs dry, I go far to fetch water
The forest has gone, how far to fetch firewood
One I take to school, the other I keep near,
For the one yet to come, I stand in a line
To take a shot from a needle.
You could hang from the beams, but I cannot
Therefore all this—
I cannot tie a knot around my own neck.
I will sow cotton again. I have got seeds on loan,
I will till the land alongside the two buffaloes,
Let's see who stops our subsidy this time!
The Wife had gone to the zilla office to check on the
interest.
The bank agent says, You are nice, your body charming!
Sleep with your door open
And the interest will be waived in a month or so!
When she returns, the Wife bathes well,
In the little water left in the well,
Then she takes a *babla* stick, shuts her door tight,
Checks the bolt again and again.
Will it be able to stop the big, brutal
Forces lurking out there?

The Man swings from the beams, his face saddened
He cannot come down if someone comes emboldened
To demand dues.

Translated from Bangla by Debjani Sengupta

Wish

Kishwar Naheed

Like Manto
I want to write my own epitaph
He had written
He was the greatest storyteller on this earth
And it is true
He was too
He wrote stories on the injustices heaped upon women
At a time when women the world over
Had not woken up to their own rights
Pakistan threw so many spatters of abuse on him that
He got angry
And began to sell his stories for ten rupees each
The spatters of abuse have turned
My dress too into undress
But I can't call myself
The greatest poet of my age
I want to write my epitaph before my death because
My sons
Busy in other countries
May not have the time, or else
May not even think of writing one
Why am I thinking of
Making myself permanent!
Is an epitaph a sign of timelessness?
In London, seeing the tombstone of Marx
You can't forget his writings, or Marx himself

There were some great poets
Who never had an epitaph
Zahoor Nazar—a great poet
He lies alone as he lived
Khushwant Singh left a will
His ashes to be strewn in the rivers of Pakistan
My heart too wants to be turned into ashes
But my religion does not allow it
A person turns to dust
After burial too
The epitaph serves to keep alive
Not you
But your age

Translated from Urdu by Rakhshanda Jalil

Coffins

Tarannum Riyaz

Mother, you had said
Go in the palanquin, bless you
Do not forget, my love!
That you will leave your new home
Only in the coffin

And if you leave before that, dear daughter
That shall not be less than a death for you

Mother, you never said
That I will have to die a fresh death every day

See how many old and new coffins of your daughter
Have collected in every corner of this 'home'
When I pass by, each of them weeps loudly
Speaks to me about the cause of death

And asks:
'How long must I die like this without being buried?'

But how can I ask you this question, Mother!
For I don't know where you are

Translated from Urdu by the author

Cannot Stoop Lower

Manju Bala

Anamika boarded an auto from Saatgachia
With her daughter Malobika
Just like an open rosebud
Her lovely face
Another woman, co-passenger, asks
Where are you going?
Lake Town. Why do you ask?
Your daughter is so lovely.
Would you mind if I ask for her hand?
My son is an officer in Sales Tax.
Anamika smiled slowly.
But one question, Sister, asks the stranger
What is your caste?
Anamika said quietly: Namashudra.
Namashudra, then it cannot be.
I am a Brahmin, married to a Kayasth
Cannot possibly stoop
Any lower.

Translated from Bangla by Debjani Sengupta

The Crystal Vase

Zahida Zaidi

The crystal vase
I had displayed in my room
With such pleasure...
Filled with red flowers
Looked so pleasing
It broke...
And scattered into smithereens
That splendour of a hundred colours
Whose rays
Had come dancing down
Into the secret chamber of life one day

....

With these bloodied hands
You'll pick these smithereens... Just think
How long will you pick them up?
Whether you gather them with your hands or pick them with your lashes
They can never be made into a crystal vase

....

Scattered on the floor lie
Blood coloured flowers
Pick them up
Before they begin to wilt
Put them in some other imaginary vase
And for a while longer keep this desolate assembly alive with fragrance

Lest all these flowers too wither away
Lest their petals too scatter
Like this crystal vase
And only thorns remain
Whose pricking will be felt
In every nerve and fibre...all your life

Translated from Urdu by Rakhshanda Jalil

The Machete

Sujata Roy

That day was Thakuma's
Shivrattir fast,
For the sago meal
My young father
Had climbed the coconut tree
Machete in hand.
Far away,
Watching the sky touching fire
Licking the houses
In neighbouring *bamun para*
He left the *kathari*
Stuck on the tree
To climb down quick.
After that...
The sago soaking in the stone vessel
The ducks in the pond, the machan
With the tender *lau* leaves
Everything left behind.
A refugee family
Crossed the Padma.
After seventy years
On a Chaitra end afternoon
Baba spoke for the last time:
'Take the machete off the tree
Gaachtar lagtashey
The tree is hurting.'

Translated from Bangla by Debjani Sengupta

Short Stories

Man

Zakia Mashhadi

Once again, the Bagmati River was in spate. It was normal for it to start swelling at the onset of the monsoon, sometimes even before its arrival. When the snow melted in the Himalayas, the Bagmati acquired a swagger. In the beginning, the angry waters looked beautiful but soon they began to wreak havoc in villages downstream.

The river and its rich flora and fauna were eternal features of the small hamlet of simple rural folk who grew maize and kept livestock. Outsiders were not uncommon as the hamlet, which sat on the border, so made it easy for people to slip quietly into Nepal if they so desired—and many of them did! Sometimes they went for shopping, while at other times for smuggling, but most of the time for crimes of greater magnitude.

Shortly before the Nepal border, women were sighted sitting outside their humble abodes knitting sweaters, shawls, mufflers, etc. over which their nimble fingers moved like machines. In the middle, they would often get up to wash a child who had just relieved herself or drain the rice, which was kept boiling on the *chulah*, or for some other housework. Finishing the job, they would return to their knitting nonchalantly. All these coarse, hand-knitted garments came into the market to provide comfort to the poor of the same kind as those who had knitted them, and so fetched a meagre profit at best. Snotty-nosed little children flitted about like birds in these settlements. Several of these inhabitants had

Nepalese features, such as soft, fair skin, slanting black eyes and slightly snub noses. With their rosy cheeks, the little children looked beautiful in spite of their poor, unkempt countenances. In the Kosi belt, such houses were common. Front doors opened in India, while the back ones were in Nepal. Borders here were porous. As for animals, they don't have any borders anyway. Whether they enter from this side (to kill) or from the other side to attack, it is of no consequence.

So it was difficult to discern whether the python came from across the border or was homegrown, whether it came swimming in the Bagmati or slithering through the dirt road used by human beings, but come it did. Snakes were not uncommon in the area. Especially in the rainy season, they were sighted hiding in the lush green grass or making their way into the jungle. Villagers avoided killing them. They said that if you steer clear of them they will not attack you, so why indulge in wanton killing? Animals being killed for food should be treated well until they are slaughtered—and that too with the least possible pain. Following this unwritten law, they did not keep their poultry in small, suffocating cages. Birds were left free to forage during the day and brought to rest in large hen coops in the evening.

To cut a long story short, the python sneaked into the courtyard of Balu Thakur and made straight for the hen coop. Balu Thakur's old grandmother, whose sight had been dimmed by cataract and memory by age, had come to collect the eggs and had left the door insecurely bolted. When something untoward is ordained to happen, favourable circumstances come up to let it happen. The snake had an easy access to the birds.

It was midnight. The sleepy, terrified birds did not even raise an alarm as three or four of the large ones got swallowed up.

In the morning, people saw the surviving birds skulking in a corner and the sated reptile sprawled lethargically across the spacious coop. Then they had another shock. Balu Thakur's 10-year-old daredevil daughter was poking her fingers in the soft flesh of the python as if it were the dough her mother made for *rotis*. She loved to sink her fingers into it in spite of being reprimanded each time.

Commotion ensued.

Balu Thakur quickly brought his axe and hacked the python into two pieces, but not before dragging the audacious child away from sight. The snake did not offer much resistance, as it had become lethargic after swallowing a couple of fat hens. In any case, pythons rest for days after they have had their fill. After some time, the village cobbler, Dulare Das, made coarse footwear out of its skin, in which Balu Thakur and his wife flopped around.

One wishes it could be possible to skin some people and convert their skin into chappals!

This had transpired two monsoons ago. In the rainy season after the next, a leopard was found on the prowl. First it was sighted on the thatched roof of Bitthal's mud and brick house. Two of his ewes had just lambed. The newly born were covered at night under a large wicker basket. It had stopped raining; a cool, moisture-laden breeze filled people with sweet languor. Trees were washed to an emerald green. Water, held in leaves, dripped in a steady trickle, giving the illusion that it was still drizzling. In the wee hours of the morning, a scream rent the air. It was Bitthal's son who had come to tend the sheep. 'The leopard has made off with one of the lambs and has injured the other!' he shouted. People gathered. No one said anything immediately, but a little while later certain things were decided as safeguards against such attacks. Barns would be made stronger; women would not go alone early in the morning to defecate behind the bushes. They would go in a group of four to five with a staff in the hands of the young and strong ones, and they would be very vigilant.

The leopard picked up a few more small animals, but there was no report of its attacking any human beings. One day, however, when a small group of women was returning from the fields, a woman who was lagging a little behind the others felt a presence. Something, someone was following her, stealthily, like a thief. The air carried an unfamiliar scent. It was neither flowers nor vegetation; neither cow dung nor any domestic animal. Bushes rustled as if wanting to say something. The secrecy of it made her hair stand on end. Was someone casting a spell? Will looking backwards turn one into stone? Still, the woman looked back. She did not turn into stone, but let forth a chilling scream and ran as fast as her legs could carry her. Others followed suit. The sudden reaction baffled the leopard who also ran and disappeared into the thick bushes.

He was one of those leopards who gets baffled by such reactions. There are lots who simply do not.

Then, like a spectre, an elephant visited the village. He registered his presence by plucking and tossing aside the newly thatched roof of Nati Panditain's humble abode. With the monsoon round the corner, the poor woman had just had it repaired. At first, people thought it was the work of a squall, but then, no squall had hit the village in recent times. But don't houses get razed to the ground, rendering people homeless, even when there are no squalls? Perhaps yes, perhaps no, but isn't life full of such riddles?

Well, eventually the villagers came to know that it was the handiwork of an elephant which had entered the hutment and, apart from Naati Panditain's roof, had demolished the banana orchard belonging to the village head. People made a plan to somehow drive the beast back into the jungle, but they had to be on their guard until it was done. 'I find Gajendra *Bhaiya*'s brother-in-law more dangerous than these animals!' quipped a young girl sitting in the group, discussing the maverick elephant. She was quickly hushed into silence by one of the elderly woman: 'Hold your tongue, girl! After all, he is your kin.'

Soon people came to know that demolishing the banana orchard was not a solo performance. The elephant had done it in collaboration with a huge sloth bear, which had made its entry by climbing the jackfruit tree standing in Noni Sao's compound. The tree had a beehive, full of honey, sweet like a young girl who had ripened under the first flush of youth. Noni Sao had sent word for Bulaqi, who was an expert in extracting honey from beehives. The bear outdid Bulaqi by half a day. Bulaqi was expected in the afternoon and the hefty bear broke open the hedge of reeds that surrounded the modest *kuchha* house at the first streak of dawn.

Noni Sao, who got up early as usual, saw him sitting comfortably, sucking honey, not in the least worried by the angry honey bees who buzzed around it in their vain attempt to chase it away. Their stings did not work because of the beast's rough, thick coat. After having eaten the honey to its heart's content, it ambled away into the thicket.

Apprehensive that the bear would come again, if not for honey then for ripe jackfruit, Noni Sao got the tree felled the very next day.

But could a daughter of the house be felled like a tree?

Along with her brother, she also went to school, a fourteen-year-old whose body had just started getting laced with the nectar of youth. Their mother packed their tiffin early in the morning in two separate tiffin boxes. Usually, a simple fare of potato-stuffed *roti* and mango pickle or plain *rotis* with some home-grown vegetables.

They were twins, but the boy was born half an hour before the girl, so he was considered older. He ate twice as much as this 'younger' sister of his. The girl often laughed, though each time she did she was chided by some elder or the other. 'He is a boy. A male body needs more energy. In fact, he eats less,' they would say.

Their mother never forgot to remind them each morning as they left for school to keep the tiffin boxes hidden deep inside the school bags, almost buried in the books. Animals have a very strong sense of smell. 'Attracted by food, they may attack,' she would say often. The other safety rule was to keep walking quietly if any animal was spotted, for animals did not do any harm unless teased or intimidated. And the third was to keep an eye on the river, especially in the rainy season, although the hutment was on higher ground and the river flowed much below it. Still, the angry waters of the Bagmati were not to be trusted. If they felt the water was rising, they should come back. The school was about three kilometres away. All the children went walking. They had no concept of any conveyance for such a short distance.

The previous night, it had rained. Trees and shrubs, grass and flowers all looked washed and lush green as if water, which was supposed to drain the colour away, had poured bucketsful of colour over them. The sun, in collaboration with the clouds, had a dappling effect on the road and trees. The magic of it all filled one with delight and a desire to dance. Intoxicated with the heady smell of wet earth and first stirrings of youth in her, the girl absorbed the fragrances of nature and started whirling.

'Now what is this?' the brother chided her in an angry tone. He was half an hour older and their mother always said that by mere virtue of being the brother he had the right and duty to keep an eye on her.

'Can't you see I am dancing? Why don't you join in too?' she retorted.

'I think you deserve a tight slap. It will set you right. We are getting late for school. We will miss out on practice for Independence Day celebrations.'

The girl chuckled as if to mock the brother. 'Independence? What is meant by that?' she said, but then fell in step with the brother on the moist dirt road that took them to school. The walk was always pleasant, as the road was lined on either side with enormous trees with a lush green canopy. The whole area was always green and colourful with wild flowers. Milk men also used the path to reach the river bank from where they took boats to deliver milk to townfolk. Their large metal containers clanged as they balanced them carefully on a bamboo pole across their shoulders. Some of them sang as they lumbered along, their melodious folk songs mingling with those of the happy birds hidden in the trees or flitting about. But these milkmen left before the school children and returned much after the school got over.

The only school in the locality, it boasted of two *pucca* rooms and a huge courtyard. The courtyard was dotted with dense trees whose shade provided some additional space for classes. There were lots of shrubs around which abounded with flowers. Peacocks strutted about; foxes stalked them hoping to steal some eggs, while monkeys swung from one branch to the other. Bulbuls sang, pigeons cooed, mynah birds flew in flocks and the parrots screeched so raucously at times that the children who called out their tables aloud could not hear their own voice. Sixty to seventy children were enrolled, but the daily attendance was twenty to twenty-five on an average before the midday meal was served. During the meal, it rose to about forty but once the meal was over, shrank back to the original or still lower. Of course, there were some regulars from the few houses where parents gave importance to education and kept vigil over their children's attendance.

These days, the number of children has gone up, as they were practising for Independence Day celebrations. Apart from fun, the incentive was the distribution of sweets after the flag-hoisting and some toffees for those who took part in sports and the singing of patriotic songs. Girls took part only in singing, so they were allowed to leave before the boys who stayed back for sports.

'Go home.' The brother's voice was imbued with authority as he was older by half an hour.

'What's the harm if I stay till you finish?' she retorted.

'No, you better leave and help mother at home,' he repeated the order and went gamboling to where the P.T. teacher was.

'Oh, how stubborn you are!' he remarked when he came back after an hour and saw her still sitting.

'Timid, not stubborn,' said she.

Actually a few girls who came to school left at where the road turned right, while this girl had to walk straight some distance. Previously, she was not scared but now for a few days she had been feeling a presence behind her. She had heard stories of leopards stalking their prey with patience that lasted for days. Then there were evil spirits. Women whose toes pointed backwards were spirits in the garb of humans. Mostly the spirits lived on trees, unseen, uncontrolled, pouncing upon unsuspecting victims. That was the reason she did not want to go home alone.

'Come on, get up now.' The brother had an edge to his voice.

Happily, she gathered her bag and got up immediately. She was not scared when he was with her. They walked hand in hand. For some distance, they had company but soon their ways parted. The two of them were left alone to cover the rest of the distance. Clouds were working their way up. A cool breeze swept across the jungle. The boy groped in his bag to feel the umbrella. It was there. Reassured, he continued walking but with a quicker pace to avoid the rains.

Suddenly, the girl felt what she had been feeling for last couple of days. A presence. Yes, some one was there. She looked at the brother. He was walking carelessly, whistling. While groping for the umbrella, he had dropped the hand of his sister.

The grass whispered, the wind grew stronger. Behind the swaying trees, she felt a shadow flitting across.

'*Bhaiya*, snake; there is a snake!' she alerted the brother.

'Nothing is there, you little fool. Walk faster. It is about to rain,' he chided her.

She felt someone breathing down her neck, making her hair stand on end. '*Bhaiya*!' she wanted to shout with all her might but the voice got stuck in her throat; her whole being felt like lead. During this fateful moment, the brother had moved a few more paces away. The girl, as though in a trance, turned as a reflex and the piercing scream that could escape her lips now, was also a reflex. But this was not a leopard that beats a hasty retreat because a girl has screamed. He tightened his hold on the girl, turned left and disappeared in the dense cover of the lush green trees. But before doing that, he had not forgotten to give a hard kick to the boy who had stopped short because of the screams of his sister. He fell face down, while the girl wriggled in the arms of her tormenter like a small fish in the large beak of a stork.

In the midst of a clump of trees, some entangled vines had made a kind of canopy under which the elephant had cleared the overgrown grass and some of the long and twisted branches, creating a small niche. Sitting there with the bear and python, he was eagerly waiting for the leopard who finally appeared with the girl on his shoulder. They screamed in delight.

All at once, heavy droplets had started falling. The boy gathered his courage and, forgetting his aching bruises, ran like one possessed. He did not stop till he reached home shouting, 'Leopard has taken her; leopard has taken her!'

People came out with whatever they could lay their hands on: bamboo pole, axe, scythe spade, anything. Sami, finding some use for the rusted sword that hung from a peg in his hut and had been useless for ages, ran with it.

The python tightened his coils around the slender 14-year-old body of the girl. She quivered and found it difficult to breathe. Suddenly, as if by a miracle, she found her voice. Perhaps the surprise had taken over the shock. 'Aren't you Gajendra *Bhaiya*'s brother-in-law?' she mumbled.

The bear was baring his ugly teeth; his smile obscene. 'Yes, and now your brother will be our brother-in-law. Of all four of us,' he said with glee and squeezed the girl as though she were a honeycomb. After a while, when the leopard struck her with his paw, her slender neck slung to one side but he licked her up with his rough, greedy tongue. After all, she was all of fourteen and the first charms of youth had started descending upon her.

The elephant trumpeted angrily, 'You bastard, she is dead.'

'She had to die. Didn't she know Gajendra *Bhaiya*'s brother-in-law?'

'But then what is left for me? I, too, had been stalking her for days and giving you her whereabouts.'

'Dead or alive, what difference does it make? Isn't she a woman? Besides, a little life is still there. She seems to be breathing and the body is warm.'

The elephant wrapped her around his trunk and tossed her like the thatched roof of Nati Panditain into the pit dug by brick makers and filled with water from the monsoon rain.

The search party found the bloated body after three days. A policeman asked the brother, 'Are you sure you saw a leopard?'

'Not very clearly. It was like a shadow flashing in front of my eyes. Then I fell face down just as I heard my sister screaming,' replied the brother, sobbing.

'Doesn't seem to be the work of a leopard or any other animal, for that matter.'

They hauled out the body. 'Apparently, it's a man or men to be exact,' commented one of the policeman.

'At least four to five,' their senior said.

After the due formalities, the body was handed over to the kin and finally consigned to the flames. When the battered and now also decomposed girl yielded herself to the crackling, all-consuming fire, the inconsolable father threw himself on the wet earth and wept aloud. 'Oh, why had I warned her only of animals!'

Translated from Urdu by the author

The Forestland

Selina Hossain

The smell of tender bamboo shoots cooking with shrimps wafted to Chandana's nostrils as she stepped into the courtyard. Ma's lunch was going to be delicious! She must eat two plates of rice and sleep soundly in the afternoon. That day, she meant to overeat; she didn't know why.

But lying in bed, tossing and turning, she could not sleep. Nowadays, she didn't. Most nights, she lay awake. Constantly, she heard a rustling near the walls of their hut. Ma got angry when she heard that.

'What noise? I don't hear them.'

When Bandhanirani got angry, Chandana said in a quiet cold voice, 'How will you hear anything? You were asleep.'

'Of course, I was. I am not haunted by ghosts.'

'Yes, they haunt me.'

Chandana felt furious, really angry. She felt like stamping the spectre beneath her foot. It was impossible to tell Ma about it. She would feel ill if she heard what really troubled Chandana. As long as she did not know, she would be at peace. But how long? Chandana's heart felt solid with pain, she was sad for Ma. But she would protect Ma from all hurt as long as she was able to.

That evening some Bengali settlers came to the house. In the light of a hurricane lantern, Chandana was preparing for a college exam the next day. The boys saw Bandhanirani in the courtyard and asked, 'How are you, Aunt?'

'What do you want, my sons?'

'Nothing. We just came to see if Chandana was home.'

'Yes, she is home. She has an exam tomorrow.'

One of them guffawed and said, 'What exam? She loves politics more than her studies.'

'Let her do what she wants, my son. My daughter has a good head. Her results are always good.'

'Not only a good head. Everything about her is good.' Some of the boys sniggered, some laughed out loud.

Chandana came out of the room, holding the lantern aloft.

'Why have you come here to laugh? Get out, get out. Or I will take a broom to your backs.'

'Oh, why are you so proud?'

'Will you leave or not?'

'You have learnt very well the manners of the Lieutenant. You must be close buddies.'

Chandana took the hurricane lantern in both hands and held it up high. As she prepared to throw it, the boys backed off and ran away. But they made a number of crude comments as they went.

Bandhanirani was upset. 'What were they saying, my daughter?'

'Don't pay any attention.'

'How can I not? I heard what they said.'

'Ah, Ma, I have to study. I have an exam tomorrow.'

Chandana took the hurricane and, with heavy feet, went back to her table. But she was unable to concentrate. When she held her head in two hands, she heard Ma on the verandah, weeping softly. Chandana felt so unhappy. As she scribbled on her notebooks, she wrote in big letters, 'Chandana, who played and laughed in the forestland, now lives in terrible times.' Chandana understood that the Lieutenant wanted her.

Like a spider, he would spin a web and she would be an insect caught in it. It was not fear, but an uncertain future that gaped wide like a mountain gorge. If once she slipped, it would mean sure death. Chandana came outside and stood behind the hut. Far away, she could see the army camp. The gun-toting sentry was also visible, like a dead tree, expressionless, unblinking. The only work that he was capable of was firing that gun.

Chandana looked at herself. She could not see herself wholly—her neck, shoulders or her back. Nor her body in front except her breasts, stomach, thighs, her feet and, in the language of the Lieutenant, her 'gorges.' Her anger increased. The man had crossed all limits. She prayed she would have the strength one day to snatch his rifle and use it to break his head. Surely, God had given us life and given us the strength to take that life? The Lieutenant's voice echoed in her ears: 'I will enter your gorges and look at the forestland, the sky. Lying there I will see the birds and the mist. If you don't behave yourself, I will tie you to a tree; you won't be able to move.'

Chandana ran near the water. She had to control her anger. She had to see her own face to do that. She could not see that part of her body without outside help. Had her face disappeared? She could not read her eyes. The lines on her forehead, the frown between her eyebrows that could express anger or love, even those were outside all that she could see. Then there were the jaws, the chin, the lips—what about them?

Chandana shouted for Ma.

Bandhanirani left her cooking to come running. 'What is it, my daughter?'

'Today is Baba's death anniversary.'

Bandhanirani paused. In a low voice, she said, 'I know.'

'I won't go to college.'

'I know.'

'I won't eat.'

'I know. Will you write? In your diary?'

'Yes.'

'And what else will you do?'

'I will kick that dog Nurul Haq's ass.'

'Will you be able to?'

'I will. You see, I will.'

'Come inside now.'

'You won't see me home today. I will go to campaign for Bijoy *Kaka*'s election. We will have to make sure he wins.'

'Can an independent candidate win?'

'He can if he is honest, hardworking. What is burning? Can't you smell it?'

Bandhanirani smelt the air and ran towards the kitchen. Chandana looked at her mother, and turned her eyes again towards the army camp on the mountaintop. She remembered the day Baba died. She was fifteen. After starving for two days, he had died slowly, vomiting blood, eyes dulled, body convulsed on the floor. All those memories no longer made her angry. Her eyes no longer became cloudy, rain no longer fell, the blue mists of the mountains no longer surrounded her. A pair of boots floated in her mind's eye. She saw bootlaces tied on the mountaintop. Those laces were tied round the neck of a girl from these mountains. The dead eyes were like marbles, white and still. A little while later, the body would be thrown into the mountain gorge. The bootlaces were strong enough to hang someone. That was the military.

Chandana gnashed her teeth in anger. Some of her thoughts were fashioned in words, some changed the look in her eyes, some changed her face to such an extent that she was a different person then. That was something she had not known herself; it was what others told her often. She could not see the whole of herself, like the water that did not catch her reflection entirely. The moss, the insects, the grains of sand and mud in it hid so many things. Her father had said, 'My girl has shining daggers inside her eyes. They flash fire.'

Her brother, Nilua, had said, 'Just like your axe, Baba.'

Dipost, youngest among them, had laughed and said, 'Her eyes contain many other eyes within them.'

All of them had laughed together.

That laughter had not lasted long in their house.

One day, her father, Gunjarlal, had set fire to a pair of boots in their courtyard.

Chandana was a little girl of ten. Gunjarlal had gone to the forest to cut bamboos and had seen a soldier raping a girl. When he had taken his axe and chased the man, the soldier had run with his boots dangling from his hands. While crossing the stream, one of the boots fell in the water. The man had not dared to stop to retrieve it. Gunjarlal had salvaged the boot from the water and had brought it home, holding it up at one end of his axe. He had told Nilua to get dry sticks from the forest.

'I am going to burn this,' he had said.

'Why, Baba? Throw it away in the forest.'

'Na, I have to burn it.' Gunjarlal had taken a long pull at the bamboo hookah he was smoking.

'I will burn it from hate. Hate.'

'Can't we tie the man to a tree and show this hate?'

'Yes, we can. Then split his head with this axe.'

'Why don't you do that, Baba?' Chandana had wrapped her arms round her father's neck.

Tired and depressed, Gunjarlal had felt his sadness sink deep within him. He had said, 'Then they will burn down our village. Kill all of us. We don't have any weapons, they do.'

Gunjarlal's anger had come down as tears. Chandana had seen the helpless cry of a man reverberate against the far mountains, and a wave of anger had swept over her body. She had said, 'Baba, I will rouse our people to fight back.'

Gunjarlal had gathered her to his heart. She sat on her father's lap that day and had seen the flaming fires lick at the boot. The air had filled with burning leather. Many, many people had come running. They had put in more twigs in the fire, in anger, loathing, despair. The fire had burnt strong.

Within a month, Gunjarlal's family had paid a price.

Bandhanirani had gone to the mountains to collect wild potatoes. The middle-aged woman was gang-raped by the soldiers. Before they left her, they kicked her with their boots and broke her waist bone. Bandhanirani had lain unconscious next to the stream.

Gunjarlal was coming home after cutting bamboo in the forest. When he saw someone lying there, he did not recognise her at first. He had thought he would have to set fire to another boot. In deep anger, he had thought this time he would set fire to a pair, and with it the rifle as well. But when he came near the stream, he did not realise how the load of bamboo fell from his head, or how he came to lie upon his unconscious wife. His hands frantically traveled all over her still body—searching for the forestland, the mountains, the sky and the closely standing trees; he tried to find them by touch. In an instant, his childhood and his middle age merged into one; in his mind's eye he saw thousands and thousands of army camps mushrooming in their Lalyagona village. The one at Uluchhori or the other one at Kojoichhori were not enough, more were needed. More and more camps: only soldiers would live there and not a single human being. Were the soldiers human too?

The next moment, Gunjarlal's hands stopped at Bandhanirani's breasts. A torrent of water came down the mountains and filled the stream. Gunjarlal watched the rushing water, heard its torrential sound with deep emotions: as if he was young again, in love again, as if drunk with love he had watched keenly his unfamiliar body after the first copulation.

Gunjarlal did not know how long he sat there. He felt in all the forestland there was not even a mild stirring of wind. The sun was standing still too—as if it had lost its way. The birds were falling one by one from the dead tree branches. What else was happening? Gunjarlal had looked around like a dumb man. He heard many voices. Many mountain people were talking somewhere far away, but they were not gathering wood, nor were they in their fields, *jhum* farming. The women had left their looms and were searching for dead bodies in the river. All their loved ones had gone to war. Nobody had returned.

By then, Gunjarlal's tears were ready to flow, and he felt a cry come up his throat, but no tears came. His anger blocked his sorrow. Gunjarlal looked in wondrous surprise at the savagely wounded breasts of Bandhanirani. His anger grew as vast as the forestland. With his axe, he split the bamboo pile in one instant. Then he picked up his wife and washed her in the water from the stream: he washed away the blood, the pieces of grass that clung to her body, the dried leaves, but the marks of the demon's paws remained. Gunjarlal gathered the strewn clothes and wet them in the water too. He gathered some leaves and holding them in his fist, he scrubbed Bandhanirani's body clean. Time and again, he thanked his God for giving him water: extraordinary water with which we shared all our sorrows. He knelt, as if he was praying, and soaked his head into the water as well. He wrapped the clothes around her as she lay in the water. He stroked her hair away from her face and softly caressed her swollen lips. He did not know what else he could do, so he slung her over his shoulders and brought her home.

Chandana was alone at home and had come running. 'Baba, what has happened to Ma? Who has beaten her?'

'The tiger mauled her.'

'The tiger!' Chandana was taken aback but she had not asked any more questions. She did not understand the man-woman equation of bodies but neither did she believe in tigers. She sat next to her mother, weeping.

The boots had broken the bones. Bandhanirani could not stand up for six months. Even now she walked with a limp. She had never told Chandana what happened that day, but Chandana understood now.

Bandhanirani finished cooking early because she wanted to go to the market at Marishya. She came out of the house with a *gamchha*; first she would go for a bath in the *chok*. She saw Chandana and said, 'Oh you are still here?'

'Ma…'

'What happened? Will you have a bath and then eat? Aren't you going out?'

'Na. Ma, do you still have that pain in your back?'

'Yes, it's so painful sometimes I can't sleep. When your father was here, he'd give me a hot oil massage. Now…it's so painful.'

'Is it only your back? Or Baba's death?'

Bandhanirani shook her head. 'After that day your father lost his health, and my body…'

Suddenly she realised what she was about to say. She walked quickly to the *chok* and dived into the water. She swam underwater and came up far from the bank. Chandana did not wait for her mother, but started off in the opposite direction. She could hear the slogans from Bijoy *Kaka*'s campaign. The Pahari mountain people were out in a procession. She ran to catch up with them.

Halfway, she came face to face with the Lieutenant. The man spread out his arms and said, 'Stop.'

'Is that an order?'

The Lieutenant laughed loudly.

'I am not afraid of you.'

'Why should you be? You love me.'

Chandana laughed mockingly. 'Love? Love is a wild boar. It grunts like one.'

The Lieutenant stamped his boots on the earth. 'If you don't behave, I will hang you at the end of this rifle…'

Huh! Chandana ducked and ran without looking back. The stamping of the boots, Ma's pain, her desire to hide underwater: they followed her, but she stopped after a while. The procession was ahead and as she began to run again, Sohail appeared from the road on the right. When he saw her running he called roughly, 'Hey girl…'

'Girl?'

'No?'

'I study in Kachalong College. And you?'

'Your love?'

'Love?'

Sohail roared with laughter.

'Dog.' Chandana picked up a stone at her feet, ready to strike.

'Say a few words of love, Chandana.'

'You dog.' Chandana threw the stone. It flew within a few inches of Sohail's head. When Sohail started walking towards her, Chandana picked up another stone quickly. She was ready for a scuffle. Everyone at the Lalyagona village, Bengali or Pahari, knew that Chandana was not someone to give up. She would always stand up against injustice—she might lose or win, but she would never give up. Before the fight could begin, they saw a group of Pahari people coming down the road. They had finished work in the forest. Sohail quickly hid behind some trees. Chandana threw away the stone in her hand.

One of the men came near Chandana and asked in a rough voice, 'What is happening Chandana?'

'Give me your axe, *Kaka*.'

'What will you do with it?'

'Give it to me.'

'I understand. Someone has made you angry. Come, let's go home.'

'*Kaka*, can you stop my anger just like that? I will split that dog's head.'

'Come with us. Calm down.'

'No, I will be late home tonight.'

Without giving them another chance to say anything more, Chandana ran off. One of the men looked at her disappearing figure and said, 'That girl is our hope.'

'I forget all my pain when I hear her speak,' said another. 'Maybe we won't see it, but our grandchildren will—all our villages, all our lands restored to us one day.'

The Pahari men spoke of hope as they walked together. They had not realised that their sorrow could pour out suddenly one day in their own words.

Chandana addressed the meeting. 'As long as true democracy is not established, women will remain in chains.

Today the Bengali rulers are oppressing us, tomorrow when the Pahari bourgeois come to power they will oppress us.'

Every day, Chandana discussed all these and more with her best friend, Kalpana. When she looked into Kalpana's eyes, she never forgot a word Kalpana had once said. Kalpana's courage flickered within her as well. Again her voice roared with words that she had learnt from Kalpana: 'In the hills of Chittagong, Pahari women are daily raped, molested, kidnapped and oppressed by the army on the one hand and the illegal settlers on the other. Their own people keep them confined within traditional society. The real truth is our women cannot get freedom without Pahari people getting their right to self-rule. If women are to be free from oppression, that can only happen through women's movement. Our freedom rests on the freedom of our men as well. So all of us have to fight together to achieve self-rule.'

Slowly, Chandana's voice faded. Kalpana was not present in the village at that moment, but she was stringing Kalpana's words deeply into the hearts of her people. The words grew deep within her. She felt that with each of these words, she was watering the roots of all the trees in the forestland with tears. With each teardrop, they would grow a tree, its branches would spread through the mountain slopes, the valleys, the plains of the land. The small trees would grow bigger and bigger—till the army left, till the settlers stopped coming, till they stopped stealing their *jhum* harvest, till they stopped cutting down trees and loading the trucks, till they filled the rivers and streams with the song that was life, till then. She stopped for a few moments and then raised her voice again, 'Where is the place where every moment, day and night, people are crushed by a terrorising army? We want to be free.'

'We want to be free,' roared the people of Baghaichhori. Chandana's voice was no longer limited to the borders of a village. Chandana now walked with giant footsteps all over the land.

A little later, she said, 'I am now Kalpana Chakma. She has taught us these words, "Don't keep us in darkness any longer, let us see." Come, let us all say that again.'

Chandana was going to the Marishya market with her mother; she would go to college from there. She held her mother's hand tightly. Her mother had told her the day before Lieutenant Nurul Haq had come looking for her. He had threatened Chandana with dire consequences.

Chandana did not say anything. Instead, she changed the topic.

'We didn't have paved roads when I was a child, Ma.'

'Yes, your father had so much trouble going to Marishya market to sell paddy. They had to walk on forest roads. A fox bit him once.'

Chandana laughed. 'Thank God, that Lieutenant was not there, he could have bitten Baba. That dog, Nurul Haq.'

'Ssh…Chandana, talk softly.'

'Kalpana has taught us to talk loudly, Ma. She has asked us to wake up. Tomorrow, she will be back from Rangamati. We will work together for Bijoy *Kaka*'s election.'

Bandhanirani did not answer. She sat under a tree to rest. Her back was hurting. She could not walk easily.

'What is it, Ma? Shall I bring you some water in an *arum* leaf?'

'Na, I don't want water. If I lie down the pain will go away.'

Bandhanirani lay under the tree. She closed her eyes. Chandana broke off a branch and fanned her. Ma was sweating profusely. Each drop of sweat looked like a small hollow of water, like the *chok* of her forestland—the small water-bodies that filled with lotuses each spring. With a sigh she said, 'This paved road was made for us to use, Ma?'

Bandhanirani kept her eyes closed, 'No.'

'You know that too.'

'The road has been made for the army and the settlers. Haven't you seen the army trucks go by? The mountains echo with their sound.'

The wind played with Chandana's hair. She said, 'Like a promise, we have to gather everyone together and keep on fighting.'

Bandhanirani suddenly sat up. Stretching her hands she caught her daughter's shoulders and said, 'If they kill you!'

'Let them. I am not afraid of death. I have only one fear.'

'What is it?'

'If there are no longer thousands of Chandana, Lalbihari, Kalindi, Kalpana, who will take my place when I am gone…'

'Yes there will be. Thousands…'

Chandana laid her head on her mother's breast. Sitting under the tree, looking at the far mountains, a deep sigh flew from her lips. She felt she could smell the burning boots; from every courtyard, in every village, the smell wafted up to the sky.

The election was the day after. The campaign ended well past evening. Chandana's home was two kilometres away.

Suparna said, 'Don't go home today. Stay back.'

'Na, I have to go back to Ma. However late it may be.'

'You will go alone?'

'Alone. Who will come with me? There has been no time to tell my words of love to anyone.'

The elders said, 'Don't go back in the night. You will have to come back again tomorrow. Aren't you going to work in the election booth?'

'Yes, I will, *Kaka*.'

'They are keeping an eye on you after that day's speech. VDP Commander Nurul Haq is a sycophant.'

'I will feed that dog to other dogs. Wait and see.'

'Don't walk the roads tonight, my daughter.'

'The road is my own. Every insect and every tree knows me.'

Laughing, Chandana began to walk up the dark road.

She would run—a long run that would reach her home. The next instant, she thought she would walk slowly. She would count each step as she walked in the forestland. In this land, every inch of space belonged to her. Among the dense trees, the moon played hide and seek and in the empty plains, it lay down large against the sky. Chandana stopped walking. The moon said in a soft whisper, 'Chandana come with me. We will spend the night talking. Tonight sleep will not come. Stay with me, Chandana.'

She began walking. The narrow path snaked between the mountains. The sound of crickets filled the night air. Chandana walked on, murmuring, 'Crickets come home with me. We will talk all night long. I have so much to say to you.'

From far away, she heard the stream. How she loved the sound of water! Chandana began to run and then stopped, 'This forestland is ours. In this forest, our ancestors made their first homes. We have made this forest habitable. Why should others uproot us and take over? Do they not know that our ancestors tended each tree of this forest? Each root carries the touch of our women. The roots now hold together the soil. The mist hanging on mountain tops have wrapped lovingly around the bodies of our men as they cultivated the land; in its virgin touch people have dreamt of making the land arable. The streams and rivers sang their lovely songs to rock my people to sleep. Each and every blade of grass, each insect, wildflower, bird and beast, each of our dwellings—*tong-ghar, macha-ghar, keyang*—every inch of this forestland belongs to us. To nobody else! We will have to drive them out. We will have to take away their weapons and make them understand that their deaths are in our hands. When I finish this, I will be able to tell Debobroto, 'Now I have time to tell you my words of love.'

He will smile and say, 'Really?'

I will say, 'Let us bathe in the stream and walk to the *keyang* to tell the priest, Here we are.'

Debobroto will smile some more and ask, 'What will the priest say then?'

'He will take one look at our faces and he will know we have come to ask his blessings.'

Oh what happiness! Chandana ran and reached home as if on wings. Bandhanirani was sitting outside waiting for her daughter. Chandana hugged her and said, 'Ma, here I am.'

'Come inside. Eat something.'

'Na, Ma. I won't eat anything now; I drank too many cups of tea.'

'Will you sleep?'

'I will write in my diary.'

Bandhanirani went inside but not to sleep. Her back was aching. In her mind's eye, the pain brought back that day. She did not want to remember that day. She had shut that doorway in her heart with a big stone. When she saw her daughter, she saw how she was growing—courageous, obstinate, her heart aching for her people. Bandhanirani's courage came back then. She loved being next to her daughter. Slowly, her eyes shut in sleep. She murmured in her sleep, 'The night is lovely in the forestland!'

And the lonely night deepened.

Chandana shut her diary. She yawned and stretched. She was not sleepy. Tomorrow Bijoy *Kaka* had to win. If he won, there would be someone who would talk about what mattered to them. What noise was that? Chandana listened carefully. Human footsteps, sound of boots?

Was it the Lieutenant? Chandana looked around. In the light of the hurricane lantern, the room was in shadows. Ma was asleep, so were Chandana's brother and his wife. Chandana was not afraid. She only gnashed her teeth and murmured, 'I have just one prayer to God. Let this forestland be mine.'

They broke open the door, ten or twelve of them. In the torchlight, she recognised some of the faces, the VDP Commander too. Chandana shouted, '*Khobordar*! Don't come a step nearer.'

Nurul Haq laughed out loud. He pointed the rifle at her and said, 'I will hang you at its end and take you.'

She tried to pick up the chair on which she was sitting. Some of the men caught hold of her, gagged and blindfolded her. She could not shout. Two men held her hands. Not the end of the rifle, but human hands picked and carried her high in the air.

Outside, the darkness was dense.

She heard animal cries coming from human throats. She heard boots crunching, from all corners of her forestland. They came nearer and nearer. Under their onslaught, the forestland lay crushed. Her breathing quickened. In that impenetrable darkness, she understood at once that the trees, the animals, and the people of the forestland lay dying.

Translated from Bangla by Debjani Sengupta

The Seventh-Month Baby

Sadiqa Nawab Sahar

This time, the rains lasted till December. By the time they stopped, the weather suddenly turned cold. One morning, I left college at 11:30. On the way back, I got off the paved road and walked to a small, unpaved path and, passing through a narrow alley, turned towards my house.

'Today, I will reach home early and rest for a bit before the cleaning woman comes,' I was thinking when I saw a man and a woman, by no means young, walking towards me in the lane. The man was wearing a grubby, white *kurta-pajama*. The woman had a light orange, striped sari wrapped tightly around her waist. A gentle smile on her clear complexion looked pleasing. The two were talking as they were walking along. I saw the man holding a cloth bundle in his hands. I thought I could see a newborn baby in it.

'*Arrey*, where are you taking this tiny infant? Whose is it?' I asked them. Those days, one heard many stories about baby thieves. 'Show me!'

The man and woman stopped. The man lowered his palm and showed the infant's face. A tiny angel was looking unblinkingly at the sky. A chubby nose, big eyes, dark pink lips, a fair-complexioned newly-born...

'Is it a seventh-month baby?' I hazarded a guess.

'Yes.'

'Where are you taking it?'

'She had the baby at 1 AM last night,' the man said, gesturing towards the woman with him who was wrapping a muffler-like cloth around her ears.

'Was it born in the hospital?' I asked.

'No, at home... We just took it to the government hospital for a check-up.'

'Is everything all right?'

'The baby is weak; they have said it has to be kept in glass.'

'Is there no incubator at the municipal hospital?'

'No.'

'What then?' I was both surprised and saddened. There are so many small villages and hamlets all over the country; what must be happening there? The thought began to trouble me.

'The doctor discharged us and sent us to the hospital in front of the bakery,' he answered.

'Sitaram Hospital?'

'Yes.'

'Why didn't you go there?'

'The lady doctor there said it would cost 2,000 rupees per day.'

'How many days will you have to stay there?'

'Fifteen.'

'...'

'The lady doctor told us to deposit thirty thousand rupees. "I will hand you a perfectly healthy baby in 15 days," she said.'

'Why didn't you keep it there then?'

'Who has the money?'

'What do you do?'

'I used to pick scrap.'

'What do you do now?

'I buy old newspapers and junk.'

'What does she do?' I gestured towards the woman.

'She used to pick through rubbish earlier...now she begs...I tell her not to but she doesn't listen.'

'How many children do you have?'

'The elder daughter is married. The second one is ten years old...the third is five.'

I was lost in deep thought.

'All right, do one thing then,' I couldn't quite understand how to help them. 'It is so cold and the baby is so tiny...it isn't right to walk around like this.'

My mind wasn't working properly. I was trying to say something and saying something else.

'Take him home. How else will he survive?' My words and my manner of speaking must have, no doubt, seemed odd to them. They gaped at me. I was embarrassed that the baby was barely a day old and I was talking about it not surviving. I averted my gaze from them and stood there and thought.

What should I do? What good does it do to make empty talk about humanity? If I do nothing, the baby will really not survive. What should I do? The thought of those generous people who do social service began to race in my mind.

'I will try and do something,' I said to him. 'Give the baby to your wife to hold in her lap and make her sit against this wall. And you come with me and see my home. Then, take your wife and child home and come to my house...by then I will see what I can do for you.'

The two of them began to consult each other.

I walked ahead a little. Turning back, I asked, 'What's your name?' It had suddenly occurred to me that I had not asked their name.

'I am Yusuf and this is my wife, Sabira.'

I was feeling very sorry for them.

***

'I want to help this child.' I reached home and called my husband.

'So go with them to M.G.M. Hospital in Kamboli... Have it admitted there, Farida Madam!' He laughed.

I stayed silent. He sensed my mood and said, 'Give them the address of the hospital and send them there with some money.'

'Will they be able to go there?'

'Do I have to tell you that too?'

'Our municipality is a Class A municipality in Maharashtra. Yet there isn't a decent hospital here!'

'Why? Haven't you seen the open ground in front of the government hospital? There's a sign there announcing the building of a hi-tech hospital on that spot.'

'It hasn't been built yet because of bribery, no doubt!'

'Work was stopped after the murder of an engineer.'

'Why don't businessmen like you build a nice hospital? People have to travel seventy-odd kilometres to get medical treatment.' He was taking the whole thing so lightly that I was getting angry.

'Then it will be a private hospital, won't it? And there are many such hospitals...the ones you call stone-hearted. The ones that are here are of no use to the poor, isn't that right, Farida Madam?'

I remembered one of my old students, Sundar, who worked as a ward boy in a government hospital. I called him and narrated the state of affairs.

'Sundar, these people are very poor. Even at a government hospital there will be some expenditure. Their state...'

'I'll tell you what to do...send them to me. I will have a letter written for them and the child will be treated free of cost at Ali Bagh government hospital.'

'What sort of hospital is it? Does it have an incubator?'

'Yes; in fact, it's famous for it.'

'There's no need to get the baby, is there?'

'The letter will only be given after checking the baby.'

'They have only just brought the baby after a check-up from there...well, never mind, I will send them to you.'

***

By about half past noon when Yusuf returned after dropping his wife and child home, I told him in a somewhat complaining tone, 'You took very long, *Bhai*.' Then I wrote Sundar's full name and designation on a piece of paper and handed it to him.

'Now go home immediately, take your wife and child and go to Ali Bagh government hospital. Take a letter from Sundar, the ward boy, and come straight to me. Take some money from me for the travel and other expenses and go to Ali Bagh.'

Yusuf left. I felt like going with him to help him but I was helpless. I had to prepare food after returning from college and clean the house with the maid. I couldn't think of lying down in my bed before 3 or 3:30 PM at least. And then my nephew was visiting for some work and was going to eat with us.

After lunch, I put the leftover food in a smaller dish in the fridge. I was giving the used plates to the maid when I suddenly remembered, 'What a strange man! It's almost 3:30 PM and he has still not come back.'

I called Sundar.

'Madam, I waited for him and then I went to have lunch.'

'He hasn't come yet?'

'No.'

'Give me a missed call when he comes.'

'Would you like to speak to our dean?' Sundar asked.

'Yes, I will.'

When I explained the matter in detail to the dean, she said, 'We don't have the facility of an incubator; it would be best to take the child to the Ali Bagh hospital.'

'You have your own hospital too, don't you; does it have an incubator?

'Yes.'

'What are its charges?'

'I can't say anything right now. My husband has gone to Nasik. He is the paediatrician. He will know.' The dean was possibly trying to get out of treating the destitute patient.

I called Sundar again at six in the evening. He said, 'I was about to call you. He has just left from here with a referral letter for Ali Bagh hospital.'

'Good! But he came so late?'

'I stayed back so late only because of you; else I would have left long ago.' He tried to press home the favour he had done.

'Thank you, Sundar.'

He was pleased and said, 'I told him not to take an ambulance; it will cost him around one thousand rupees. If he takes the bus, he will reach in a hundred rupees only.'

'All right, so if he has left your hospital now, he will come straight to me...but it's getting colder. Should I send him now or tomorrow morning?'

'Send him in the morning.'

'Thank you, Sundar!' I was relieved.

That evening, Yusuf didn't come to me. I began to get increasingly restless. I felt like going to the shanties in Kajuvadi in search of him. He had said that his house was at the foot of the hill, just a few houses down. I looked at the watch. It was 9 PM. His house was ten minutes away, but I didn't have the courage to go at this time of the night. At night, slum dwellers are known to drink when they return home after a day of hard labour. I could smell the stench of strong country liquor in my breath and persuaded myself not to go there. Then I began to think if I could call a student from Kajuvadi or one of my husband's labour to go with me and find out. I thought of a girl who was in the final year of college. Actually, our college was right next to the hill of Kajuvadi. Kajuvadi falls in the forested area. Being part of the government out-bank area, whenever there's any plan to erase the slums the women from these hutments go to the local political leader with their rolling pins in hand and he assures them he will not allow their homes to be erased. No one knows how people have ownership proof for these houses built all over the hill. There must be around two hundred and fifty houses here, some of which are *pukka* houses. The ones with the *pukka* construction came together and got a toilet made for their private use; each family keeps one key to the toilet. For the others, there are municipality lavatories next to the old police station near the highway. In the mornings, you can see little children happily relieving themselves on the slip road that runs past Kajuwadi along the old Mumbai–Pune highway.

'What shall we do?' I asked my husband. 'It is very dangerous to keep the child at home all night. Why don't we admit him to the private hospital nearby that is charging two thousand rupees per day for the incubator?'

'There's no use. The private hospital will find some excuse or the other to keep the baby for several days longer. After all, you have a fat wallet!'

***

I woke up at 3 AM the next day. I was restless. The child should be rushed to the hospital as soon as possible. How happy I would be if I could see that child grow up and studying. In our society, the birth of a son is cause for such joy. These people are so strange! Did the man not know that his wife was expecting? Could he not have saved some money in the past nine months?

I resolved to go to Yusuf's house first thing in the morning. I will give them the money and ask them to leave as soon as possible. But by the time I had done some light exercises, made breakfast for my husband, got ready myself and had a cup of tea, it was 7:30 AM The first bell rang at the college at 7:45 AM.

'If I go now, I will be late for college. And then I will first also have to look for the house,' I said to myself.

The fourth lecture was part of the foundation course. There were only two boys present during the class. It was the inaugural day of the sports championship and the games were about to begin. Outside, a crowd of students were standing against the railing of the playground. In the course of the lecture, I mentioned the seven-month-old baby to the two students in my class and said, 'These people are careless. I don't know if they will even know which bus to get into. The two of you come with me, put them on a bus to Ali Bagh and only then go home.'

And so I set out for Yusuf's house with the two boys in tow. It wasn't difficult to find the house. Yusuf had told me: his house was at the first right turn as you enter the small gate of Kajuwadi.

I asked a woman who was combing her hair in one of the huts, 'Where does Yusuf live?'

With the comb in her hand, she paused for thought and asked, 'The one who had a baby the day before?' She asked by way of clarification and then pointed ahead with the comb.

I moved forward. This part of Kajuwadi was extremely dirty. The huts were huddled close to each other, separated by narrow, dingy lanes. On this side of the hill, three women and some children were sitting in front of a hut. Since they didn't have a *bindi* on their forehead, they seemed Muslim to me; in all other respects they were a symbol of a shared culture. A short distance behind them was an open-air bathroom made of dirty old straw matting; someone seemed to be taking a bath in it.

Dirty water from the soap was coming out from beneath the matting, finding its way between the rocks and falling down the slope to disappear somewhere down the hill. Close by was a shed with a tin roof and bamboo walls. I cast a quick glance inside the shed; its walls were plastered with mud. Some gleaming utensils were neatly arranged on a piece of wood nailed to the wall. Beneath it was a mud stove with some dried wooden sticks lying beside it. A cot was placed near the door; behind the cot hung a curtain on a piece of string which divided the hut into two parts.

'How is the baby?' I asked the woman who was sitting with one leg bent at the foot of the cot and whom I recognised as Sabira. But instead of Sabira, one of the women sitting outside the hut—a fat woman with curly hair and dishevelled sari—answered, 'It's dead.'

'When?' I gasped in surprise.

'This morning at 6.'

I nearly sank to the ground with sorrow.

'Why didn't you come home yesterday?' I asked Sabira. She stayed silent but the curly-haired woman answered, 'These people lost the letter from the hospital. And they couldn't find your house.'

'Couldn't find my house? But I had shown my house to Yusuf!'

'Yusuf had told Sabira the way to your house but she couldn't follow it. He wanted her to go, but she...'

'Who are you?' The fact that the curly-haired woman was constantly butting into the conversation made me think she must be a member of Yusuf's family.

'I am also Yusuf's wife.'

I was surprised.

'Show me the baby's face,' I said as I entered the hut with slow steps.

Sabira nudged aside the white sheet covering the baby on the cot and showed me its face. My heart beat fast. I had seen this baby's face yesterday; was it expressing a desire to stay alive longer? Its plump cheeks had sunk. Its fair complexion had darkened... How insensitive this neighbourhood was! This must be happening here all the time!

'Where's your husband?'

'He has gone to tell Hafiz*ji* to make reparations for the burial,' said the curly-haired one.

Suddenly, a two-year-old boy came racing towards the curly-haired woman. She was sitting with her legs spread out. She saw the child and immediately crossed her legs. The child ran and lay down on her legs. And she began to suckle the child. She had no thought for her clothes. I began to feel a bit embarrassed. I stood between her and my students.

My heart said to me, 'I wanted to spend some money to save the baby; that money will now probably be used for her burial.'

'You will need money for the burial,' I said to Sabira as I withdrew some money from my bag.

'No, no, don't give any money for the burial. I am sitting here.' I was surprised when the curly-haired woman said these words.

'Are you the first wife or the second?'

'I am the first.'

I looked at her carefully. There seemed to be no real difference between both of Yusuf's wives—in age or appearance.

'You didn't have children? Is that why he married again?'

'My husband fell in love with her. And so he ran away with her. At that time, my first baby was still in my womb.'

'If not for the burial, at least let me give her some money for other expenses,' I found myself taking permission from the curly-haired woman to give some money to Sabira.

'I have money for my baby's needs. It is my right. I had told her and my husband: "I am ready to bear all the expenses. Give me the boy; I will take him to the hospital." But she didn't listen to me. As though the boy would have grown up to support only me!' I could see the pride of being the senior wife on the face of the curly-haired woman as she spoke to me.

I took out a five-hundred-rupee note from my purse and tried to put it in Sabira's hand. A man emerged from behind the curtain. He resembled Yusuf; I assumed he must be his brother. He stretched out his hand and tried to take the money. When I pulled my hand back, he gestured to Sabira to take the money as though he was trying to say that he would have taken the money and given it to Sabira and that I had misunderstood the situation.

★★★

With slow steps, I returned home. I found the maid waiting for me at my door.

'Did you have the baby sent to Ali Bagh? He will be all right now; babies become fine once they have been put in the glass box,' my maid said as soon as she saw me.

'The baby died.'

'When?'

'This morning...at 6.'

'He would have survived if you had admitted him to our local hospital, wouldn't he?' I was surprised when I heard her say this. The guilt intensified in my heart. I panicked and like any other housewife, I took recourse in my husband.

'*Sahab* had told me not to get too involved in this matter. "If something were to go wrong at the hospital, these people will blame you," he had said. What can I do if *sahab* had forbidden me?' I answered her and freed myself from the sense of regret.

Translated from Urdu by Rakhshanda Jalil

Bonodurga Slakes Her Thirst

Jhumur Pandey

Having touched the green hilltops, the wintry sunlight slipped through the branches of the leathery jackfruit tree and the crevices of the bamboo hut, before falling diagonally on Bonodurga's lean face. Her hair had not been oiled in ages and yet the soft soothing rays made them shine. Nobody knew what time of the day it was...the dew was still dripping until a while back—*tuptap-tuptap*. It had been dripping like that since last night, on her heart and memory, on the bamboo pole and the matted jute quilt. She ran her bedewed hands caressing fields of mustard, potato and peas, until she stumbled upon a lotus pond. There were no lotuses right now. Do they ever blossom in winter? While collecting lotuses for the goddess Bishohari, her brother had died from a snake bite. The little boy was still lying amidst a hundred lotuses. Oh dear! Even then, he was holding on to a thick stem of a full-bloomed lotus. Water trickled down the cheeks of Bonodurga. One drop. Two drops. Three drops. It kept rolling. The bird has just started to tweet—*kich-mich-kich-mich*.

Her throat was parched. If only she could drink some water. But not a single limb was capable of moving. Even the eyelids did not open. She had been silent for days. Now and then, Phuchoo's father, Nimai's mother and Sanatan's brother came to check whether the heart was still beating... no...rather if the heart hasn't stopped beating yet. At least they kept an eye, they who were not her kin while those who were related by blood, social norms and soul... The bird called out again. Again, those lotuses…huge ones. Jogoi was rushing with the long stems. He was dark with spiky hair. *Le Le*, he cried.

She held the myriad flowers in her tiny hands.

'Do you want to eat the stem?'

'Give me one.'

'No. No. Come to the enclosure. We will eat there.'

'Let's go.'

There was a strange pain in her breast, the throat dry. But who would give her water? There seemed to be a few perched crows sitting near the door. Bonodurga could sense their smell and the sound of their wings. They seemed to be discussing something. A crow was electrocuted sometime back. Hundreds of fellow crows had gathered to mourn it, leaving everything aside. On the other hand, when the brother who worked in a city confectionary was crushed under a lorry, not a single person offered him water. He was lying on the ground for hours. Crows and human beings; human beings and crows. Bonodurga's long breath got stuck on its way out. Someone was coming. Must be Phuchoo's father. These days, Bonodurga grasped everything by their sounds. There was a rasp of a door opening. It was made of bamboo. Just shut, unlocked. Who was peeping in? Phuchoo's father, it seemed.

'Please give me some water.'

He came closer.

'Water... O Phuchoo's father, give me some water.'

He went back. One could hear the door closing and the footsteps fading. Didn't Phuchoo's father hear her voice?

'O Phuchoo's father! O Phuchoo's father!'

Bonodurga called out again.

The crows had flown away. Some people were walking by the low mound. Did they have cattle with them? Yes,

Bonodurga could hear the steps of the cows. After building a hut in the forest, she had kept a calf that later became pregnant. She was named Mangala. Who had kept Mangala? Did she give birth? Ah! How's the calf? Must be giving milk by now. Once again, her long breath got stuck while exhaling from the mouth. The bird was calling again. Some people were coming that way. There were footsteps of two people—Nimai's mother and her grandson, Shudhonno.

Nimai's mother bent down to listen to Bonodurga's breathing.

'Can you please give me a little water?'

'She is still alive,' said Nimai's mother.

'Let's go then.' Shudhonno made a move to leave.

'Can you please give me a little water, Nimai's mother?'

Oh no. Nimai's mother was leaving, closing the door after her.

'Nimai's mother? O Nimai's mother…'

Oh…

Tears rained down Bonodurga's lean cheeks. They made their way past her neck and breasts, stumbling into her navel. 'Oh Mother! Ma… O Ma, give me a little water, *jol deo go, Maa…*'

Ma was getting water from the brook. She was carrying a clay pitcher around her waist, three aluminum containers over her head and all the washed clothes in one hand—the very image of Jagat Janani, the Mother of the Universe. Her reddish hair reached till her waist. She was very fair. After all, she was the daughter of a Sahib. She used to pick tea leaves and manage Jagat Bauri's household, giving birth to five–six children, when one day all of a sudden, she fell down dead…

The crows were cawing again. The sun had moved away from her face. Bonodurga could smell the marigolds and their leaves. Did they grow in the courtyard? She had planted the branches before the *puja*. A pity she couldn't see them bloom! Kauwa or Hajari? Or was it the marigold variety called Krishna *genda*? She had seen white marigold in Krishnababu's house. She had thought of getting a branch but couldn't manage. Else…

The common iora called out. That bird didn't tweet at that time of the day. Where did it come from? For days, Bonodurga had chased the yellow bird leaving aside her all her work. Two of these birds had built their nest in the bushes around the Kali *thaan*, the site of worship. Soon enough, the eggs were laid and incubated by the female while the male searched for food. One day, two healthy chicks hatched out. They always kept their mouths open for food. Someone was coming again! Seemed like Babu's second son, the only one amongst five who came now and then. After the death of Babu's wife, Bonodurga brought them up as her own, leaving her own household. People initially described her as Babu's maid, then 'mistress' and finally wife. Buying household stuff from the bazaar and cooking every day took a toll on her body. The money that she had acquired after selling her father's land was used to repay the loan taken against Babu's house. After Babu's death, his sons threw her out. They, for whom she had done so much…tears rolled down her cheeks. A pity…where had she stored all the water in her eyes? The boy entered the room followed by Nimai's mother. Was she outside all this while?

'Cover her with the quilt. Must be cold.'

Bonodurga smiled to herself—What was cold? What was warmth? They had all become irrelevant to her. Was today the last day of the month of *Poush*? Or was it gone? Who knew?

On the day of the *Porob* festival, Bonodurga along with her mother and the neighbours would bring water from

Dhaleshwari river at night. Lokkhimoni family's *Tushu* idol would then be paraded and garlanded. Having eaten *pitha* and hopping from one house to another with Tushu, Bonodurga's feet would start aching. Her maternal grandfather sang:

Who is that girl
In Chhotobabu's *kotha*?
Wearing diamond cut bangles
What pleasure does she seek?

In Babu's house, Bonodurga had learnt to make various kinds of *pitha*. Ah! Babu's first son was very fond of the one made of flattened rice. He would nag her to make it during his holidays. Some time ago, during such an event, Nimai's mother had covered her with a quilt received during last election. But what about some water? If only she gave Bonodurga some water. O Nimai's mother, Nimai's mother! Tears trickle down her cheeks once again. The two left murmuring something to each other. The bird called out again. The year was a little colder with a cool breeze blowing as well. The blanket smelt of something strong, the smell made her dizzy. Once upon a time, people were scared to sit on her clean, crisp bed as she was known for her cleanliness. She learnt so many things in Babu's house, so many ways of cooking and habits of living. Mother was equally tidy and kept the rooms, courtyard and enclosures neat and shiny. One day, her father had stumbled and fallen flat on a freshly caked courtyard, shot in the back for asking bonus for tea garden workers. Mother, having bathed and rolled a few *rotis*, had just started making tea with salt. Ah! The aroma of hot *roti* was still fresh in the room as Bonodurga sat looking at the first rolling of the hay in Durga's *thaan*. The hay was yet to be covered with clay to make the idol. Father hadn't eaten for two days; he had been so busy arranging rallies and meetings. In that hungry state, he had fallen. The *ishtikutum* bird called out again. Someone was playing a *dhapla* somewhere. She could hear women singing. Was someone getting married? Oh yes, Phuchoo was supposed to get married in Rupachhoraye. She remembered everything now. Was it Phuchoo's turmeric ceremony? Bonodurga had been applied turmeric and mustard paste for almost seven days. Such music and revelry! Her young heart had swum with a flooding excitement. But Bonodurga had no pleasure of a household of her own. Her *morod* used to stay with a woman from another caste. One day during her pregnancy, her drunk husband had kicked her tummy so hard that the room became a pool of blood. The band seemed to be coming this way. The bird kept calling. It was as if the bird's call and the music mingled and became one. She wished someone removed the quilt; it felt so heavy. Some people had given it to her during the last election. Apparently, many quilts were distributed. But she didn't have to vote; it was already cast. Since the last few elections, Bonodurga hadn't been able to vote. Some other people did. The music faded away. They must be going to the Kali *thaan*. Oh god! Wish someone removed the quilt. Would anyone come that way? It was very heavy, making it difficult for her to breathe. Once, Bonodurga had the strength of a demon and courage as well. During the last election when Shuhashbabu's son was being beaten to pulp by a few goons, Bonodurga alone like Maa Durga...and when Shobori's daughter was being...the bird called out again. Apparently, Shuhash's son is now in America, while Shobori's daughter just got a job in a school. She had so much strength, but now she couldn't even lift the quilt...the long breath stuck near her throat again. A few tears trickled down her cheeks. The little girl was swinging her legs while sitting on the lychee tree.

She was jumping from one branch to another. Hey, throw a few below.

All her childhood friends—Sulochona, Shakuntala, Phoolbashia—each one of them stared with mouths wide open.

Wait. Wait.

The myriad sweet-sour tastes still played about inside the tiny mouth. The bird called out again. If only someone could remove the quilt. Such a pain!

One could hear the song of the shaman, the *ojha*. Was a boat being worshipped somewhere? Last time it took place in front of the burning *ghat*. The aged woman, Rami had dreams and had begged throughout the year…only Goddess Manasa amidst all the deities…a pity… It seems that the bird had now perched on the roof of the hut. The little girl ran through the meandering road that resembled the hair parting of a fashionable girl. The common hill myna was whistling. Was the breeze laden with the aroma of *chhatim* flowers? Who knew? No, the trees were loaded with *shimul* and *palash* flowers.

'Hey, why are you running so fast?'

The girl abruptly stopped.

'You have grown up, haven't you?'

Arrey, it was Jogoi. Jogoi had enrolled in the police force. That was the last time they had spoken. They had never met after that. The pain in her heart stirred up again. When she was pushed out of Babu's house, Phuchoo's father had helped her construct a small bamboo hut in the forest. She lived comfortably there. Since then, they call her Bonodurga (Durga of the forest). Her real name was Umashashi. Ma used to say that the name was given by someone. Ah, couldn't remember now. Having lost their landed property, Phuchoo's family, too, built a house near her. There trains now whistled away, tearing apart their ancestral land. Mangoes, berries, jackfruit, areca nut—what a pity! There were olive and plum trees too. Squirrels jumped on top of a pomelo tree. They expected a lot of money; the MLA Sahib had assured them compensation. But where were the banknotes? The owner was supposed to get 80 per cent and the rest would go to others—the case was still stuck in court. The hill myna called out. The yellow iora called too with it. Babu had a myna in his room. It used to bathe in turmeric water. It would call out to the ducks. There had wafted a smell of hyacinth bean leaves and flowers. Oh yes, he had planted them in the scorching summer of last *Jaistha*. As soon as the plants grew up an arm's length, he had made a *machan*. The white and purple flowers were visible after the *pujas*. The *machan* must have filled with the beans now. But she couldn't see it, could she? *Arrey*, how was Majhli? Was she alive? She hadn't returned since she went to Kolkata with Krishnababu's sister. After two years, when her mother wanted to see her, they said she had run away with a rogue. Did she really elope? Some said she was sold off to human traffickers. A pity! Majhli, her sister, had just left her knee length frocks to start on saris those days. Her big grey eyes had stood out of her face framed with golden hair. There was a lockout in the tea estate. People had been starving to death or why would her mother send her girl away so far? Bonodurga's heart wept for one look at Majhli. Tears trickled down her cheeks in a fresh stream. Someone was coming...again. Who? Didn't seem anyone familiar. The person was speaking to Sanatan's brother.

'She is my wife, I am telling you the truth.'

'Your wife?'

'Yes. Married wife.'

Bonodurga overheard the words carefully. Yes, the voice sounded familiar. It was her brutal *morod*, her husband. But her breast brimmed with joy. The brute remembered her after all. He has come to see me for one last time! Tears trickled down the cheeks. If only she could open the eyes, if only she could get a glimpse of his face.

'How much land is here?'

'Never mind, how much; it's *khas* land.'

'Yes, but some are encroached upon too. And brother, I also heard that some acres in Shiling are in her name.'

What was the man talking about? Lands and possessions? What a shame! The tears from her eyes rolled down and stuck to her cheeks. She remembered the time when she got the land in Shiling, thanks to Krishnababu. Once she had cultivated rice on it. Who knows who was doing it now? So, this greedy brute had come for the land? Disgusting!

Yes, the land was there. But—

'But what?'

'But Babu's second son may claim it.'

O goddess! That's why he comes by. Such selfish desires! Oh Ma, where do I hide my face!

'Other people have taken care of things here, so it's natural they have a claim too,' says Sanatan's elder brother.

Bonodurga's tears dried. If only she could puke…she felt dizzy. Even when they could afford only boiled potatoes and her little brother used to cry out in hunger all night, her father had returned a bag full of money to the police. People had told him that this must be a dacoit's loot and so he should keep it, share some with them and live like a king. Upon hearing this, her father had closed his ears—Ram! Ram! Once mother, too, had returned the gold chain of a memsahib. The birds were calling out again. The quilt received during that election reposed heavy on her body. She could smell incense sticks, flowers too. Was there a *puja* at Badhsha *thaan*? She used to go to their annual *puja* with her father. The place was a dense forest then. She had eaten *khichdi* on a banana leaf. So many tigers and deer...what a pity. There were rabbits and colourful birds too. Wild duck. Once a cheetah had jumped just five feet across Bonodurga. It didn't harm her and had crossed over to the lake on the other side. Out of fear and anxiety, Bonodurga had stood still for quite some time. The birds were calling out again. Who knew what time it was in the afternoon. The aroma of the incense warmed her heart. A cuckoo called out. She heard its call for the first time that year. The quilt had moved on its own. Had they all left? No, they were arguing over something outside. Bonodurga could now see everything clearly. Someone had peeled oranges and poured the juice into her mouth. Oh dear, the ants were marching towards her mouth. For how many days had she been lying like this? There were ulcers on her back and feet. They were still fighting. No, nobody was crying. Maybe there would be noise of splitting wood and bamboo sticks. Bonodurga laughed aloud for quite some time. There was so much greenery, flowers and forest outside. Ah! Such wonderful scattered clouds in the sky. A flock of wild ducks flew away. A guinea fowl too. The white-breasted water hen was nibbling on something. The aroma of the incense from Badshah *thaan* had softened the air. She could smell the mustard flowers too. After all, the field below the hills had already turned yellow. Her heart felt rather light. Bonodurga breathed uneasily and her entire body yearned for water. An intense yearning! There was a brook right after one crossed the hill. Throughout days and nights, the torrent raged. Stepping into the cascade, Bonodurga would scoop the water in her twin palms and slake her thirst to her heart's content.

Translated from Bangla
by Lipika Das and Rajorshi Das

Roll of the Dice

Aniqa Naz

None of us wore masks. That meant people could see us right away. But we were protected by being indistinguishable. There are lots of people with faces like ours in this country. And even if some of us have distinguishing features that could be remembered, no one had the presence of mind, or the time, to remember well enough to identify us later. The way I see it, when people are experiencing extreme fear, that's all they remember—the fear. And anyway, even if they do remember something for a little while, how long will that last? Not long at all. Progress is what you call it when you remember new things quickly and forget old things just as fast. People who don't are like dinosaurs and will soon become extinct. At least that's what I read in my Matriculation science book.

None of the three of us wants to get killed. At least not until the right time. By the right time—I don't mean fifty-five; middle-aged—that's the fate of most people born in this country. What I mean by the right time is as long as I can help myself to the things I want when I want and as much as I want. That's why sometimes I'm forced to forget even myself. Life is beautiful. Even I know that.

Okay, moving along, most of the time our hunts aren't all that planned out beforehand. According to the traditional laws of hunting, we target the weakest in the bunch, the people that can't put up much of a fight, except our approach to hunting people is different from animals, because we keep the status of the prey in mind. We look for prey with enough resources to be worth our while. You don't just know this from facts. Experience is important too; it heightens the sixth sense. 'A hunter has to be one hundred percent alert.' That's Kashif Virus's motto. He's the most educated of us. He got a B.Com degree, and he also shows us fun stuff on the computer.

Now, take that bus. So many buses drove by that bus stop. But we wanted the kind of bus that had fewer people with more stuff. These new buses, the AC ones that run in the city. The Green Lines and the Blue Lines. Not every Tom, Dick and Harry can afford those buses. Those are the buses for us. People who can afford more expensive fare are definitely going to have more stuff. Eleven o'clock in the morning is the perfect time—there's not a large crowd, and the passengers can easily be shaken down.

Mukhtar Tarzan signalled for the bus to stop. One good thing about these buses is the bitches actually stop at their bus stops. You don't have to go running after them. The bus's automatic door opened and we got on one after another. There were about ten women sitting up front and around twenty men in the back. The conductor was sitting by his ticket machine. You go up to him to buy your ticket. Conductors have it really easy, man. There was a chilly feel to the bus; it didn't smell of *paan* spit or anything. Those buses don't jolt along at every step either. Money buys the good things in life. People are always saying you shouldn't lust after money, but who lusts after money? All us suckers want the good things in our lives. Everyone lusts after the good life. If you could get whatever you wanted without money, why would anyone go around robbing banks, stealing cars or snatching purses? Yeah, even I would go watch that what-d'you-call-it, you know, the kind of fancy dancing Sheema Kirmani does. I'd spend my vacations in a rented hut on the beach, have a nice car, a new model of mobile phone, a nice brand of clothes, shoes and perfume, Reynolds sunglasses. But! You need dough—bits of paper printed with Quaid-i-Azam's face on it—for all that stuff. Not even the pimps will let you sneak into the red-light district without it.

I looked around one more time. How many of them would remember my face? Would the old guy in front? Hardly! He was probably trying to remember where to get off the bus. Or would that self-important man, sitting there wearing trousers and a shirt? If I were sitting in his living room a month later wearing Benetton pants, a cotton shirt and film-star sneakers, asking to marry his daughter, would that asshole recognise my face? Bet you he wouldn't recognise me even if he wanted to.

The three of us went and sat in the empty seats. I went over to the ladies' section. Women's faces look so dumb when they go pale. I love it when they say, 'Oh brother, oh son, have mercy on us,' and when they get all scared and call me 'rascal' and 'bastard'.

Kashif Virus went to the furthest back seats and Mukhtar Tarzan went to the middle section. By this point I was getting kind of excited—like I had fire running through my veins instead of blood. Three of the women were wearing gold bangles. There aren't as many women in gold bangles as there used to be, but you still come across a few. Go ahead and buy gold if you're into it, but what's with these women who think they look so amazing wearing gold? One woman was sitting at an angle to me and I could only see her hands, which were heavily decorated with *mehndi*. She wore lots of red glass bangles on her wrists that were jangling around, but the sound just didn't have that magic jingle gold bangles do, and she kept twisting the ring she wore on her right hand. Just one ring! This woman is of no use, I thought. The ring was set with a gemstone. Probably won't get much for it. But she was wearing a *burqa*, so it was possible she had gold jewellery on the inside. My heart pounded with excitement and I felt the fire in my blood.

Tarzan went over by the conductor with his head down. At first, the conductor looked pleased to see a customer. He probably thought mistakenly that Tarzan had come to buy a ticket. He wore a short-sleeved shirt and trousers, and was looking very respectable himself. The jerk probably didn't make more than four thousand rupees a month, but somehow he was able to look pretty dapper. His wife probably stitched clothing for the entire neighborhood and belonged to a community ladies' committee. His children probably studied in a yellow government school or in one of those open-format private schools that crop up in neighbourhood homes, where the teachers earn a hundred rupees a month. The conductor looked at Tarzan and smiled, and then suddenly his expression changed to a grimace and his eyes widened. He might not have seen a TT pistol before today, but seeing one on television or in a movie and seeing one right in front of you are two different things. I totally get that—the first time I held one in my hand, it was like a volcano erupting inside me. That little piece of metal made me feel so powerful. And nothing gives you a bigger high than power. I knew then that I could have anything, anything that important people have. It was all mine! All of it! I slowly imbibed its coolness through my palm.

The conductor looked at me and then he looked at Tarzan. Three TTs. He whimpered. The bastard probably wet himself. Tarzan quickly turned toward the men's section and I rushed over to the women's section. He yelled, 'No one make any noise! Quick, quick! Put whatever you have in here.' He went running around, pushing a bag in front of everyone. The passengers must have been astonished as well. What just happened? That's just how it goes, people. Fate, goddamn fate—it's got you trapped. 'Mobiles, mobiles. Take off the watches too.' I could hear him wheezing as he spoke. That jerk wheezes more than he works.

As expected, the women got all tearful when they saw me. Okay, for one thing, I just don't get women. They could be happy or sad, frightened or doing something brave, but the bitches always weep and carry on no matter what's happening. One time my dad threw me out of the house because he didn't approve of some of my habits. What was I supposed to do? I had nowhere to stay, so I spent my nights on the roofs of tombs. Whenever I heard a sound and woke up suddenly at night and looked around, I'd see women up to their black magic: one would be wiping away her tears as she poked a small effigy with needles, another would be sobbing while she filled a little bag with earth from a grave. Women love drama, whether it's on Star Plus or something they cooked up themselves. So in a way, we were actually helping these women out.

The driver, the moron, turned toward me suddenly, like he was going to curse me out: 'Hey there, son of a *hijra*, what are you doing in the ladies' section?' But then he saw the piece in my hand and shut up. Maybe he suddenly remembered that *hijras* can't have kids. I didn't even need to tell him, 'Keep driving; don't even think of stopping!' because he completely froze. But I did it anyway, to impress the others: 'Keep driving! Don't stop the bus, moron!' By now, the bus was already on Sakhi Hasan Road. The road was as clear as a bald man's head—that's how good our timing was. I quickly emptied the purses, or rather, grabbed them. I made the women take off their bangles and rings. Two wore *burqas*.

There was no time to argue with them. I just took whatever was visible. When I got to that woman who was twisting her ring, she looked at me questioningly, as if to say, 'Are you going to rob meeven me!' I didn't pay much attention to her meek face. It was showtime. 'Give me your purse. The purse. Hurry.' She handed over the purse with trembling hands—and the ring—as I motioned toward her hand with my TT. 'It's my wedding ring.' Dumb bitch, women go seriously nuts for jewellery. I was just thinking I ought to smack that red-lipsticked mouth, when someone screamed behind me, 'Help! I've been shot!' I was on high alert now. Our plan had been to shoot no one unless absolutely necessary. A woman screamed, 'Oh, Allah, please help us!' At times like these, people always think of Allah. Why should Allah care about all these opportunistic and thoughtless people? If God listened to all the opportunistic requests, opportunists would be the only believers. I get that. So anyway, that woman with the ring turned around immediately, and screamed as though she was the one who'd been shot. 'Kamal!' she screamed and jumped up immediately. Our work was pretty much done. The boy who'd been shot had fallen to the floor, clutching his stomach. 'Help, I'm dying!' He was writhing. Everyone else was cowed. That must have been why Virus shot him. The sound of a shot really lets the air out of people. Try shooting a bullet sometime and see what happens. Pow! Hisssss!

I shoved the woman back into her seat with the butt of my pistol, but she just kept squirming. Then I screamed to the driver, 'Hit the brakes!' I knew it would take time for him to come to a stop, but I took a shot at the windshield, right near his head. The bus went completely silent. The windshield shattered into a web of cracks with a tiny hole in the centre. The driver stared at it fixedly. 'Help, help!' But outside, the world went on its way, lost in its own concerns. There was a boy who kept staring at a girl. A man was looking at his watch. It was actually bad timing for us. A traffic cop was stopping a minibus. He had ten rupees coming to him. No way were these jerks about to help the driver. 'Hey, hurry up!' I shouted. Now we'd stop faster than fast, I thought, and that's what happened. Near the KDA Quarters intersection, the bus stopped. The driver pressed the lever and the door opened. Just like Ali Baba's cave. Open Sesame. All three of us jumped out. Now the quicker and further we could get from that place, the better. The three of us were definitely thinking this and possibly the stupid passengers as well.

Someone was driving toward us on a motorcycle. 'Stop him!' yelled Tarzan, out of breath. One of us ran over and waved a TT at the driver. We were running with our TTs in our hands. The motorcycle driver had noticed. He thought he was being clever and sped up. Can a motorcycle ride faster than a bullet? He chose the wrong moment to test that hypothesis. His experiment failed. But the asshole fell over in a weird way so it would have taken us too much time to separate him from his motorcycle. Someone was approaching us from behind in a car. The moment Tarzan motioned to him with his pistol, he stopped the car, got out and ran like he'd seen a ghost. Fear of death is stronger than fear of ghosts. A ghost might turn out to know you and then go easy on you, but fucking bullets don't recognise anyone. They're blind, like the law. Virus grabbed the steering wheel and we went careening through back alleys and streets. During this time, we divided all the loot up into two bags. I took charge of one, Tarzan the other.

Near Faisal Bazaar, we ditched the car and continued on foot. After a bit, the three of us got on different buses. That night, we emptied out all the purses and took care of them first. As long as we held onto them or had any identification on us, we were in danger. We could be identified at any time, so we had to unload them right away. All together, we had more than stuff worth two-and-a-half lakh rupees. Everything we did yesterday took no more than half an hour—the time it took to travel from one bus stop to the next. Now that's what you call a cakewalk.

That night, when the red wine had gone to our heads, we started talking about everything that went down. I asked Virus, 'Dude, I get why you killed the guy on the motorcycle. But why'd you blow away that other guy, the one on the bus, you asshole?' 'He was getting cocky. That's why I smoked him.' He carelessly took a gulp and waved his hand in the air. Tarzan laughed so hard he clutched his stomach. 'Ha! You smoked him!' The thing is, if you want to survive, then be flexible, be submissive, be a coward. If you get cocky, you'll get blown away yourself. 'Geez, Virus, you're a bloody genius!' I clinked my glass against his.

The next day, we learned from the newspaper that the guy on the motorcycle was a *maulvi* on his way home from teaching kids the Quran. Trash out, problem solved. If the bobblehead had lived, he'd probably have taken four wives and had six kids with each. Then they'd have grown up and become extremists and then the government would have had to put a huge price on their heads. And if he hadn't married four wives, the bastard would have opened a *madrasa*, basically a terrorist-manufacturing factory. So actually we did everyone a favour. And we went ahead and helped ourselves to the reward. All you idiots should thank us. Go ahead and say it, 'Bravo! Bravo! Bravo!' 'No problem, just doing our duty.'

And the boy on the bus, he passed onto the next world as well. We all have to go there someday. Poor guy just had to go there first. Anyway, to hell with people like him! If a man can't give his wife gold bangles, what's the point of him living? Turns out, that woman, right, the one with the ring—she was his wife. The two of them had been married just a month before. I remember her big, round, *kajal*-lined, questioning eyes. Just like Aishwarya Rai. She was quite pretty. It won't be hard to get her married again, and until then, she can distract herself with the ring. A gem-studded ring. It's possible she'll get a nicer ring the next time round, and gold bangles too.

In four or five days, we got all the stuff taken care of. Wandering around from alley to alley, hunting down each target—that's dangerous work and much less profitable. We got as much in one go as we'd have gotten after a full week of hard labour and much more danger. And we're the heroes of our own full-time drama. That would be pretty hard to pull off in this country otherwise.

Whenever I have money in my pocket, I have to go see Zuby. Zuby is my girlfriend. The word 'girlfriend' doesn't sound so novel anymore, but I like it. Nowadays the words 'girlfriend' and 'boyfriend' are markers of social status and liberalism. Liberalism! Every government gives us a slogan, a token of itself, just like in the movies, when the hero gives the heroine some kind of token of his affection. We got liberalism this time. The word liberalism is so useful too. Words like sin and virtue seem old and cruel in comparison. But what does that have to do with me! I want none of it. They're wrapped up in their own little worlds and so am I.

Anyway, if you're a young guy and you don't have a girlfriend, you haven't lived! I'm not in love with Zuby, and she's not my wife. Those kinds of women stifle you. Nope, she's just my girlfriend. She whispers sweet nothings to me. She's with me today, she could be with someone else tomorrow, but we won't even recognise each other then, because I'll be with someone else too. The truth is, relationships ruin everything.

That day, I took particular care with my look. A new, imported T-shirt and wrinkle-free jeans from Thailand, a new hairstyle and a close shave. I got a stylish car from Rent-a-Car. When I saw the sparkle in Zuby's eyes, I could tell my effort had paid off. I took her to the golddealer's shop and she was absolutely stunned. 'What are you staring at?' I asked her. 'Let's make it a golden day!' I wanted to surprise her. 'You're giving me a present!' she beamed. 'Yes!' 'Then get me that ring!' She grabbed my arm and pointed toward a ring set with a gemstone. I was silent for a moment. 'A ring!' I looked at Zuby. There was a golden sparkle in her big, round, *kajal*-lined eyes. I don't believe in fate, but all the same, I have to admit I felt a little anxious. What if fate couldn't tell the difference between a girlfriend and a wife and smoked me too?

Translated from Urdu by Daisy Rockwell

Fragrance

Azra Abbas

She didn't know if the fragrance was following her, or she it, but this game had been going on for a long time. Much time had passed since the days she used to get up early in the morning, and tiptoe very quietly out of her room. Her nose would follow the fragrance and she'd walk by one, two, three, four apartments, and go and stand before that one. The fragrance now went right into her nose and flowed down her throat. She would stand and stare through the crack in the door of the apartment for some time, her eyes wandering over the entire room. She'd be lost in the magic of that room—as much as she could make out through the crack. Then she'd tap softly on the door. 'Come in.' She'd open the door and tiptoe inside. She'd stare with starry eyes at the woman from whom the fragrance flowed. Smiling eyes welcomed her back. She herself answered only with her eyes. Her lips felt stuck together as when she slept.

The shimmering walls and ceiling and bed in that small room, and that woman, that room, cloaked in golden and silvery hues—it all seemed a dream to her. Everything was imbued with magic. And all around her, that strange fragrance, filling her nose, her throat, her stomach. She'd sit motionless. The woman would wander about before her in a wondrous manner wearing colourful golden clothing. She liked that woman who sat sometimes before the mirror, or sometimes on the bed. Who was she? She had no connection to her. At that age, she knew of no other relations besides mothers and aunts. Her only connection to that woman was her fragrance, which roused her from her bed every morning and pulled her there. She liked it all very much, like those dreams that filled her eyes at night when she slept.

She'd forget all about breakfast and lunch and just sit there. All other activities felt unnecessary to her. All else was useless before that fragrance. Unaware of all other things, unaware of everyone, her mother, father, sister, brother, she stayed there from morning to noon. Why would anyone remove themselves from that fragrance and go back home? But perhaps it had been necessary to return home for some reason. She had no idea how she got back home, how she separated herself from the fragrance and left. Perhaps, she had to leave.

On her return, her family would cross-examine her. Where had she gone, barefoot, without washing her face, without having anything to eat or drink? Her mother would place her hand on her head and look at her tearfully, her father's angry voice would swirl around her, her brother and sister would pull at her frock and ask where she'd been, and she would just stand there silently. After that, as on every day, she'd forget the wafting fragrance for a while in the din of their voices. She'd spend the rest of the day playing with other children and quarrelling over little things and laughing.

But the next morning, the same thing would happen again. As soon as her eyes opened, her nose would fill with that wafting fragrance. She'd feel a lump rise in her throat. She'd feel a tightening in her chest and stomach and get up. Her mother would be warming up the hearth. Her father would be scanning the newspaper. Everyone was up to one thing or another. She'd glance about once, or sometimes not look at anything at all, and tiptoe out. That same door, that same crack, that same bed, that same woman, and the flood of fragrances, the festoons of sparkling golden and silvery tinsel, and the shimmering hues all around.

Who knows how long this game went on and when and how she and the fragrance parted ways. But never again did she encounter it. That apartment wasn't there, nor those shimmering colours; every single thing had changed. She was in some other place, some other home, but that fragrance continued to fill her nose, her throat, her chest for long after. The days continued to roll by and much time passed. Sometimes at night, very late, or at the crack of dawn, that fragrance would awaken her and become a dot that wandered before her eyes. Perhaps, she herself turned the fragrance into a dot. The dot would begin to travel far from her sight. She'd set out softly after it. The dot would keep moving away. She'd keep following it. She'd emerge into the light of day before a pond, beneath a tree, silently, in a field. But in the dark of night, when all the doors and windows were shut and everyone was sleeping, the dot would expand and cloak her in a black shawl. And she'd grow upset. But no one was aware of her condition.

These moments continued to occur in different ways—and in the meantime, she learned much with her mother, with her sisters, with her female relations, with friends her own age. And so an age passed by, but still that fragrance was nowhere. It was only a memory, an idea: those colours that had settled in her eyes, that fragrance which lingered in her nostrils. And it was all reduced to a dot. Time passed, and kept passing. When she went to weddings, she would see many women dressed up, exuding fragrances, but that fragrance which followed her, or which she followed, was nowhere. In darkness, under muted lights, in shining mornings and baking afternoons—nowhere, never. Time had taught her many things, and she'd come to know much. Even after all she knew in the darkness and in the light, in the changing ebb and flow of life, that fragrance and that dot would sometimes appear before her; it would circle around before her eyes and melt into her pupils. And at those moments she felt blinded.

Then one day, when her hands, too, were decorated with sparkling tinsels, and her body was wrapped in many colours, she lifted her head amidst an incredible din and looked around. It was a roof just like that other one, walls exactly the same, a shimmering room, just like the other; everything was precisely the same. The colours danced before her eyes. Digging far back in her memory, she remembered that old apartment. Everything seemed just the same. She turned about and examined herself. But that fragrance—she breathed in deeply. There were many fragrances. They were all new, but that particular enchanting fragrance was not present. The brightness in her eyes blurred, the shimmering lights grew dim.

One morning, as she stood surrounded by those colours, someone tapped at her door. 'Come in.' She smiled and looked toward the door. Her visitor sat down on the chair by the door, dressed in a tiny frock. 'Why have you come, did some fragrance pull you here? Tell me!' The little girl just stared at her with starry eyes. 'Your nose, your throat, your belly, they're full of some fragrance, a fragrance has pulled you here.' The little girl stared at the sparkling festoons of tinsel with starry eyes. She had her lips pressed tightly together—just as she must in her sleep. She breathed heavily, her eyes wide open, astonished. 'No, no, that fragrance is not here. Why have you come? Have you been drawn here by some fragrance?'

She looked at the little girl with surprise, fear, sorrow and kept questioning her, and the little girl just stared at her with astonished eyes, the shimmering colours reflected in her pupils.

Translated from Urdu by Daisy Rockwell

Famine-Stricken Akaalu's Fish Dreams

Papree Rahman

The price of rice began to soar alarmingly, just as the flames on a dry thatched roof shot skywards. Beyond ordinary people's reach: Twenty-five, thirty-five, and then it became forty taka! There was no stop to it.

Akaalu stared at his stomach, bemused. The skin of his belly was touching the back-bone. Where was his stomach? The wrinkled hollow, touching the spine, looked more like a date palm, cut and shorn, shriveled-up, the skin stretched on the bones. What use are skins and bones, Akaalu thought. The most important thing was the stomach: that bag of skin inside which one's life resided. And one had to keep filling it up, that bag, otherwise one couldn't survive! That wrinkled bag was like a giant cavern, it could absorb whatever one put into it: cow, goat, duck, chicken, bull, sheep, camel, lamb. It rejected nothing. Everything was absorbed in no time.

Thus, when the price of rice touched forty, Akaalu began to stare at his stomach more and more. He was in a quandary and there was no solution to his problem. How did one appease hunger pangs? Side by side, Akaalu also kept glancing at Gonjera Begum's stomach, with even greater frequency and unease. While his own stomach was becoming hollow, Gonjera Begum's stomach was not touching her spine at all. No! In fact, just the opposite! Her stomach had taken the shape of a ripe jackfruit. And the sight of it sent shivers down his spine. It filled him with uncontrollable unease and anxiety.

Gonjera Begum's jackfruit-like tummy was nothing new. It had swelled up like that two or three times earlier. But nothing had come of it; nothing from that swollen-up belly had survived. That had happened in the last four or five years.

What puzzled Akaalu was that Gonjera's belly was rising at the same rate as the price of rice.

Akaalu's mind went back to his childhood. He remembered his fishing days, how he had loved that sport. And if a *taptapi* fish or two were caught in the net, as invariably they were, how delighted his friends and he would become. Holding these fish upside down by their tails, they would watch with fascination as the bellies filled up with air and swelled up to an enormous size, almost to bursting point. Yes, Gonjera Begum's belly was swelling up too, like those fish. Akaalu felt uncomfortable as these thoughts crowded his mind.

There was no dearth of ponds and tanks in Mithapukur, and Akaalu had been crazy about fishing. Whenever he cast his net into the water, a net of any kind, *khuajal*, *palajal*, *jhakijal*, he came up with plenty of catch. So many kinds of delectable fish—*puti*, *tangra*, *mola*, *chapila*; his net would be brimming, spilling over. And with those others, invariably, a few of the blackish-yellow *taptapi*, or *potka* fish as some preferred to call them, would come up too. *Taptapi* fish were simply amazing.

The kids would suspend them upside down by their tails and, lo and behold, their bellies would start to swell up until it looked like a drum. All the while, they would chant in a chorus: *Taptapi—jhinga seed! Taptapi—jhinga seed!*

Then, when the bellies were swollen to a bursting point, Akaalu and his friends would kick them with a twist of their left ankle, smash the tummies and watch them burst with a loud bang. Like mini balloons! How that delighted them!

Why and how the cruel killings gave so much pleasure to Akaalu and his friends remained a mystery to this day.

And with the price of rice soaring higher and higher, and Gonjera Begum's belly getting larger and larger, Akaalu could not help his mind wander.

Ah, he found himself thinking, if Gorjera Begum had a tail. And if one could hold her by the tail, and swing her around, would her belly start to swell? Like the *taptapi?*

As they sat down to eat, Akaalu tried desperately to banish these thoughts from his mind. Look how she gobbles rice, he thought to himself, No fish, no meat, just rice, salt and chilly! What an appetite!

Again that thought came to him: If only Gonjera had a tail! Would her tummy swell, too, like those fish? The thought came back to torture him. Look how she gobbled up rice. And how her tummy swells, he marvelled. He knew the thoughts were wicked; he tried to push them away, but they kept returning to plague him.

If only Gonjera Begum had a tail.

And even if she had a tail, could he actually hold her upside down, and would her belly swell up? And if he kicked her with his left ankle, would she die? Would the child in her belly survive?

Better to think of other things, he thought.

Who knew it would be so hard feed his wife; she with the jackfruit belly! And the unborn child! And what about his own belly? Night and day, these worries haunted Akaalu: the unborn child, his wife, and he himself. He had heard on the television that a pregnant woman needed double the amount of nourishment, in order to have a healthy baby. What was he to do? He had left his ancestral home in Mithapukur, and had come to Dhaka in search of food. And now he was facing the same problem, the same scarcity in Dhaka! It was their stomachs, his own and Gonjera Begum's, that had brought them here. But had it brought them any relief, any solution? No, not at all. The price of rice and Gonjera Begum's stomach both had grown larger and bigger.

Akaalu had pedalled all over the city, up to Bheribandh, Ashulia and beyond, all in quest of cheaper rice but to no success. The two ends just refused to meet. There was the rickshaw owner; he had to be paid sixty to seventy taka per day. How much was left? How could he feed himself or Gonjera Begum? Lentils were touching one hundred and ten taka. Cooking oil? Beyond reach! How could he face his wife?

Suddenly Akaalu was overcome by an irrational anger. He stared at Gonjera Begum, enraged. After coming to Dhaka, she had completely changed. He realised, with some horror, that she had lost all sense of feminine modesty. Not only had her stomach enlarged, so had her breasts. They had become enormous. And she didn't bother to cover herself properly, like a well brought-up woman should. She walked in a strange way, splaying her feet awkwardly. She squatted about on the floor with her legs spread out. Shameless! Even he, her husband, felt compelled to avert his eyes. Unable to tolerate this immodesty any longer, Akaalu lost his temper. No food to eat, and on top of it, this blatant exposure of her body.

'Gonjera Begum', he shouted. Have you completely lost all sense of shame after coming to Dhaka?

Gonjera was taken aback at Akaalu's outburst. She stared at him, uncomprehending. What was he up to now, she thought. Why was he creating a scene? Aloud she said, 'What are you talking about? I don't understand.'

'Well, you know,' he said, embarrassed now, 'so many men live around here. They walk about—shouldn't you cover yourself properly?'

'My, oh my,' Gonjera burst out, quite angry herself, 'Look how this half-dead man speaks! Become a proper gentleman, have you, after coming to the city? Huh?'

Akaalu's temper flared too. 'How dare you answer back, huh? You shameless woman.'

Gonjera was not to be daunted. Angrily she muttered, under her breath, 'What is there, half-dead man, what is there in this body? Tell me; what is there that will attract any man?' 'In this Dhaka city, she continued bitterly, 'all those shameless city-bred hussies have made this half-dead man crazy! Something has gone wrong with his eyes.'

Gonjera continued to berate, 'Look at the women here. Displaying their breasts! Do they cover their bodies? And those elevated shoes they wear! And he calls me, immodest!' There was no stopping her now, as she continued on and on, for had she not seen with her own eyes how these women moved around without shame, their bodies, their stomachs, their waists, left uncovered. Had she not seen with her own eyes these women wearing *belauz* without any sleeves! Exposing their bare arms. Shame! Some of them didn't ever clean the jungle growth under those arms! Shame! Shame! Hadn't her man seen these, that he was lecturing Gonjera Begum to cover her body?

Gonjera pulled her sari tightly around her body. But it was simply hopeless. If she tried to cover her breasts, her swollen belly protruded, and if she pulled the sari around her tummy, her breasts were exposed. What was she to do? The more tightly she pulled her sari around her, the more her body was uncovered, showing her pale, fair, swelling belly.

Akaalu looked away in shame. He couldn't bear it anymore. That pale, fair, belly… Dark, disturbing thoughts crept into his mind without warning. Gonjera's pale swollen belly and *taptapi* fish with their pale yellow, swollen bellies and blackish green backs. Why, Gonjera Begum's back was blackish green too! How strange, how very eerie! Because of the unnatural swelling, her stomach was white and pale. And that live jackfruit inside the belly. Would that be swelling too?

And then the awful reality—rice for forty taka! And Gonjera's appetite! She gulped rice like a crazed woman. Pulling his rickshaw all day long, he couldn't satisfy that appetite.

That night, Akaalu couldn't sleep. He could see the rise and fall of Gonjera's belly. Was he half asleep, half awake or was that Gonjera's belly talking? Was it trying to say something? In that darkness, not a flicker of light anywhere, in pitch darkness, how could he see the rise and fall of her belly? He sat up in fear.

'Have you had a bad dream, husband? Why are you sitting up in the middle of the night?' Her calm voice floated up to him, with no trace of anger, irritation or rancor.

Akaalu didn't answer. He felt a soft pair of hands gently stroking his back, his stomach. Were they a woman's hands or was it a snake? Akaalu remained silent and motionless. Was it a dream or a nightmare? And in that half-conscious state, he heard her speak in a hesitant, timid voice: 'What shall I tell you, husband, what is there to say? I know how difficult it is to even get the rice we need. But who can control the mind, its desires and cravings? I have this uncontrollable hankering: you may even call it greed to eat some fish. If only you could get me a *chaitta* fish…' Gonjera's voice broke off hesitantly.

Akaalu felt a jolt run through his body. What was she talking about? Didn't she know how expensive everything had become? Commodities were far beyond his, or anyone's, reach. And she craved fish! What was he to do with such an unthinking woman—Allah help him!

As he pedalled his rickshaw, the calm, still river stretched out in front of Akaalu. There were no waves to be seen. Since he had left Mithapukur, Akaalu knew only this river. For him, no other river existed. It stretched beyond Bheribandh, leaving Ashulia, and stretched further and further away. In Akaalu's mind, it was his river, his lost river, this road-river that lay in front of him. Akaalu had not tasted the waters of this river nor had he gauged its depth. But it was his river. He didn't know the name of this river; it could be his Mithapukur's Gobeswari or Bholamati or Dhepa or Icchamati. Every day, Akaalu passed along this river and stared into its still, dark waters. Fishermen had enclosed portions of the water with bamboo slats to trap fish. This enclosed portion surely belonged to somebody. Sometimes, Akaalu saw one or two big fish along with a host of smaller fish trapped there. Akaalu would stop and watch, enchanted. How Gonjera Begum would have relished some fish with her rice. On his way home, Akaalu bought some yams and *kolmi* leaves. Gonjera cooked it silently. Akaalu was quite content, but Gonjera's desire for fish disturbed him. He ate quietly.

Akaalu was driving along the road-river. As he drove into the dry land, the sun was fading. There was an unbearable cacophony of sound all around him. His feet became icy. The rickshaw became stiff. He had to get a *chaitta* fish for Gonjera. He had to! His wife had requested him for some fish to eat with her rice. All said and done, a wife was a wife. And she was pregnant, carrying his child. How could he go home without the fish?

Not that Akaalu had not tried, and a number of times too. He had gone to the fish bazaar and bargained hard. But all to no avail. He just didn't have the money. That son of a bitch *mahajon* was so stingy with his rickshaw. If Akaalu got the rickshaw in the mornings, another puller got it in the afternoons. The miser! That left Akaalu with no money to spare. All day long, as Akaalu ferried his passengers, he was plagued with this one thought—how to get some fish for Gonjera.

All of a sudden, Akaalu stopped short and stared at the river, hypnotised by the sight in front on him. There were no crows, no birds anywhere around him. Only hundreds and hundreds of *taptapi* fish rising from the waters! Again and again, he stared, mesmerised, bewildered. The fish were rising from the waters, their eyes pointing to the sky! Yes, they were *taptapi* fish, with blackish-green bellies. Akaalu rubbed his eyes in disbelief—were these *taptapi* fish or was it Gonjera Begum's swollen belly?

What is this, he thought. Have all the *taptapi* fish, from all the ponds, lakes, tanks, gutters, rivers, come to Dhaka?

He made up his mind. He would have to go down into the waters and look for himself.

The next day, Akaalu did not go to the *mahajon* to collect the rickshaw. Instead, he rolled his *lungi* tightly around his waist and descended into the waters. He had to check for himself. Lower and lower, he went, his hands stretched out to touch the bloated creatures. But, in a trice they vanished from view. Just disappeared!

There, in front of him, he saw the fish enclosure, fenced off with bamboo slats. He could see hundreds of fish there playfully bouncing and leaping inside. So many of them! So the rascals are all there. What was he to do?

Akaalu knew exactly what he had to do. He had to very careful. If the owner saw him, there would be hell to pay. Very cautiously, he pushed the slats aside and quietly entered the enclosure. There were hundreds of fish, so many varieties of them, leaping up, diving down, and disappearing into the waters. But no sign of those swollen bellied fish at all! Akaalu's mind went back to his childhood days. How he had loved to fish. Why, he could catch them with his bare hands.

If only he could catch one or two for Gonjera. How happy she would be. Her craving for fish curry with rich gravy and rice would be satisfied.

Akaalu found himself deep in the waters, his feet firmly embedded on the river-bed. Suddenly, he experienced a ticklish sensation on the sole of his feet. A very familiar sensation he recognised from his childhood. He bent down into the waters, chest deep. Using both his hands he caught the creature, oh a live fish! My goodness, he shouted in excitement, a live *bayam*!

Yes, a fresh *bayam* fish, wriggling and writhing in Akaalu's strong grip, desperate to escape. Akaalu held it tightly, determined to take it home.

Again, something tickled the sole of his feet. What! Another one?

Akaalu narrowed his eyes, he looked to right and left. If the owner was anywhere around, he would have it! No, no one in sight. But what to do with the one in his hand? It was so slippery, one loose grip and it would go right back into its muddy hole.

Akaalu found the solution. He held the fish between his teeth tightly. He stooped into the waters again, chest deep. Another *bayam* fish, even bigger this time! He held on to it with difficulty, its body was slippery, covered in slime. It was twisting and twitching, trying to escape with all its might. But no, Akaalu held the creature tight; he would not let it escape.

Suddenly, the fish held between his teeth slipped down his throat. Lower and lower, the fish went, into his body, lower down, perhaps looking for an outlet—a way out. It ate into his vitals, his heart, his lungs, his spine. Even lower. Maybe to come out, maybe not. Akaalu could not understand anything more.

Before he finally lost consciousness, Akaalu saw thousands of *taptapi* fish all around him, their slimy yellow, swollen bellies. Or was it Gonjera Begum's pale swollen belly? Everything was a haze, Akaalu could not make out anything.

Before finally closing his eyes, another desire overtook him. Like he would often do with the *taptapi* fish, Akaalu wanted to lift his left ankle…and…push hard on Gonjera Begum's swollen belly.

Translated from Bangla by Shahruk Rahman

Straw and Chaff

Maitri Roy Moulik

Even without looking up from the ash-covered utensils lying beside the common tube well, Rama senses Chintamoni stomping around the yard. The water from the tube well is not fit for drinking. It is salty and carries a nauseating, stinking smell. But one can make do with it for washing and cleaning. The water for cooking has to be brought from the tap on the main road. Even that water tastes stale if one is unable to store it at dawn. Pulses refuse to boil. Putting the plates into the water-filled plastic tub, Rama begins to dip the ladles, pots, glasses that have been scrubbed with ash into the water in the iron tub. After a set of cleansing, she will change the water and wash them again. Casting a side glance, she sees Chintamoni has lost one slipper. Picking up the sari end and petticoat from the foot that is missing a slipper, she says loudly so that Rama can hear, 'Who has stolen my slipper?'

Seeing Rama unmoved, Chintamoni looks towards the sky and raises her voice, 'Rascal! Bastard boy! What fun is it to hide the slipper of an old woman?'

Clenching her jaws, Rama continues to scrub her pots and pans. The old woman is trying to pick a fight. She just wants to cause trouble, swear and then make up. Can't let that happen today. She will have to make Chintamoni leave by noon. In the morning, Gana had left saying, 'I don't want to see her face when I come back for lunch.' He couldn't get himself to say that to his own mother.

'Look at this vile woman! Everyone pops off but her!'

There's a muffled laughter from somewhere. Must be Kochi amusing herself with this scene. Lazing on the ground, Runu the goat is chewing on some leaves. Chintamoni's missing slipper can be seen lying flat under her ass. The goat's hair and the slipper's colour are so similar that is difficult to locate it at first sight.

'Hey! Go away! Go!' Chintamoni shouts from a distance. Runu is a naughty animal, keeps loitering around…specially if she spots a buck. Attempts have been made twice to bring in the ram and get her pregnant but to no avail.

Chintamoni breaks a twig from the guava tree and starts poking Runu. Rama intentionally avoids looking at her. She knows the moment their eyes meet there will be a hailstorm of insults. The chewing of leaves seems to have made Runu drowsy. The prodding made her fold her front legs and sit up. Chintamoni took this opportunity to move her slipper.

'*Myago! Haigya muitya thuishey!*' Chintamoni begins to drag the shit covered slipper to the tube well area with the twig. Keeping aside a bucket of water, Rama dips the ladle and glasses into the tub of water.

Chintamoni dips the slipper along with the twig in the bucket. Rama pretends to ignore that and keeps washing the utensils. After another set of swearing, Chintamoni gives up. Leaving the gate of the fence open, she walks off. Rama throws a side glance to see the old woman leaving. Even amidst the bouts of quarrels, the old woman has decked herself. Eyes lined with kohl, a big, red *bindi* on her forehead and a long strip of vermilion in the parting of her hair. Her lips red by chewing catechu, she walks along the mud furrow along the field, cussing. Stepping on her toe, Rama checks the area around the field. Prasen Bagdi's wife is plucking pea leaves nearby. On hearing the old woman, she stops to ask, 'Oh Grandma! Where are you going, swearing like this?'

That is all Chintamoni needed. She starts to shout with venom, 'That whore is not letting me stay at my son's house.'

Prasen Bagdi's wife hides her laugh with the end of her sari and quips, 'Why are you abusing her, grandma; isn't she your daughter-in-law?'

'When did she become my daughter-in-law? God knows from where my son has picked her up! That whore and her children are now eating off my son!'

Tucking her sari in her hip, Rama comes out. Seeing her, Prasen Bagdi's wife hurriedly turns back to pluck her leaves. The old woman picks up speed. The only human on the field now is Togori's mad uncle. Clapping his hands, he begins to follow Chintamoni.

Who knows how many venomous stories that woman will spread on her way to the station! Rama can count on her little finger exactly how many days the people in the household get food on Gana's income. Her previous husband was a complete drunkard. He would beat her every now and then. For eleven years, Rama worked as a maid in people's houses to feed him. Getting food on the plate without having to work only strengthened him more. Sticks, ladles, chunk of wood, whatever he could lay his hands on he would beat her with. Once he had attacked her with a scythe at the dead of the night. He had already removed her sari, all she had on was a torn blouse and petticoat. Unable to run away, she had to spend the night in the cowshed covering her breasts. Gana used to visit them often. He was the neighbourhood brother-in-law. His wife was making life hell for him too. One day, Rama left her two daughters and eloped with Gana. Though it was only she who walked out of her marriage for good.

Gana Mallick still visits his wife twice a month. Although a bit of a dandy, the man does not drink except on occasions. He does odd jobs. Sometimes working as a labourer, sometimes as a guard. For ten days, he had sat in the market to sell sandals. Often fails to collect wages from most places, borrows money here and there. It is Rama who keeps the household afloat by working as a cook in two houses. The wages are quite meagre here compared to that in Kolkata. For two years, Rama had worked as a maid at a house in Kolkata. But she had to leave at Gana's insistence. He felt empty without her. Kochi and Shyamoli were at home making do somehow, cooking for Gana and looking after the house. But was it possible for ten- and fifteen-year-olds to cook and serve food like an adult? At last Rama had to return to Basirhat after letting Shyamoli take up where she worked. Today, Gana left right before dawn. He had been whining right from the day Chintamoni arrived, insisting, 'I can't sleep at night. Drive out the old woman!'

Since Babusona's cries disturbed his sleep, Gana no longer sleeps in the same room with Rama. He sleeps in the next room. But Chintamoni occupies that when she arrives to stay. Even if the old woman is driven out, she will come back again in two months. She is supposedly working in the same neighbourhood as Shyamoli. Like a fool, Kochi has given her Shyamoli's address. Apparently, the old woman has seen Shyamoli on a bike with a boy. Nonsense! It's a pot calling the kettle black! That woman had been sleeping around her whole life and now she is slandering her own granddaughter! Every two or three months the woman comes, gives money to her son but never a paisa to Rama. Like mother like son! Gana flatters his mother for a day or two and then schemes to cause trouble to drive her away. Rama, too, takes the opportunity to vent by cussing her. Why won't she? Has this woman ever acknowledged her as her daughter-in-law? Has she ever entrusted her with a rupee?

Rama comes out to the yard and calls, 'Kochi, where are you?'

Kochi responds from inside the house, 'Can't come now, am polishing my nails.'

'Please come! I have *shakri* on my hands; I can't go in with this. You know that is impure. Come quick!'

Kochi comes to the door while drying her nails, 'What happened?'

'Why did you throw the old woman's slipper on the goat shit?'

'So what? I will do it again! Do you know what she said? Yesterday, she touched my breasts and asked how come they are this big, with whom have you been fooling around? Mother, please don't let her in again.'

'Who am I to allow her in? It's your father. First he flatters the woman to get her money, and then schemes to drive her away!'

'You know, Gana has taken quite some money from her this time!'

'How much? Were you counting?'

'Huh! Did he let me lay my hands on it that I will count? I have only seen a bundle of hundred rupee notes! Go and see, by now he must have spent them already.'

'I'll do that later. You go sit beside your brother and do whatever you are doing. I will have to go to work once I am done washing the utensils.'

'Mother, will you return early today? Want to go to the fair.'

'With whom are you going? If your father comes to know, he will scold you.'

'I will go with him only. Gana has said he will bring some *jalebi* for you. You will have them at night, won't you?'

'Sure. If you buy it thinking of me, why won't I have it? Now go sit with your brother.'

On returning from work, Rama found Gana's van parked outside the house. This van was bought last year with Rama and Shyamoli's savings. It is not a passenger van. There is a CD player inside that plays devotional hymns. An idol of Krishna is kept over a cloth. The van is taken door to door for people to give their offerings to God. People offer rice, potatoes, money. Even if one takes it around thrice a week, a week's rice can be arranged. But Gana is too lazy to do that; he keeps making excuses of being sick and stays home. Today must be the same. Had he gone out with the van, it would have been late when he returned. Even the incense sticks before the idol are lying the same way they were before. Hearing her son's cry, Rama wiped her sweaty face and went in. Breastfeeding, she went to the next room. Normally, father–daughter bonding is a good thing for a family, but Rama somehow feels uncomfortable every time she sees Gana and Kochi sitting close together. Today, she also feels the worry. It is difficult to keep control of a girl this age. She can't be kept at home for long. She is fifteen now, yet she does nothing. Sits with her father all day, if possible. If Gana comes late, she gets angry, argues, swears, calls him names. Sometimes, she even leaves home after a fight. Gana has to go and coax her to return. Rama felt like a theatre company manager in this drama between father and daughter.

But today Rama decides to play a different role. Today she is an audience who will throw rotten eggs to end the show. Usually, the audience yells before throwing rotten eggs, almost as a warning, to alert the actors so that those who wish to leave may do so.

Rama asks in a high pitch voice, 'Why is the van empty? Where is the rice?' Both the performers ignore her. Kochi hugs her father more tightly and rests her head on his stomach. Having been fed, Babusona is fast asleep. It is Babusona who can be used as a rotten egg then. Rama takes him to Kochi and says, 'Please take your brother, make his bed and put him there.'

Kochi fears this tone in her voice. Shrugging, she takes her brother and heads to the bedroom.

Gana laughs, 'See you've made her angry. Who will give me an oil massage now?'

Rama grits her teeth, 'Tomorrow early morning, you will take the van around.'

'What will I do taking the van around? The battery for the recorder is dead.'

'You took fifty rupees the other day to fix that. What happened?'

Gana replies in a sing-song tone, 'Kochi please explain to your stupid mother that batteries don't get fixed with fifty rupees. Tell her to give me two hundred rupees and I will bring a new battery.'

Rama says, 'You can get many batteries with the money you have stolen from your mother.'

Gana seems amused, 'Listen to this stupid woman! That old woman will give me money! Whatever she gave me has gone in clearing debts.'

'I clear all your debts. Which one is this?'

'I am not answerable to my wife. Now that you've irked my darling daughter, my *choto ma*, who will give me the oil massage?'

Gana tugs the *gamcha* from the string. The string breaks. He tucks the towel on his hip and heads towards the pond.

Rama sits on the stairs. Her head reels. On returning from his bath, Gana spots a half-conscious Rama on the stairs and gets perturbed. '*Bou,* are you sick? See all these quarrels have made you ill! Kochi, please bring a glass of water, quick!'

Tired, Rama says weakly, 'Let her be.'

Gana starts to cry, 'We will be destroyed if anything happens to you, *kala bou*!'

'What's it to you? You can go back to your previous wife. You have kept that door open.'

'That is duty. Without you, *boro ma*, *chhoto ma*, what do I have in life?'

Rama's eyes fill with tears. Her drunk wifebeater of a husband used to say women have taps fitted in their eyes... be it joy or sorrow, water would start pouring. Rama would wonder what happened in other times; was there any time when the water ran out?

It was noon. Shyamoli was usually alone in the flat at this time. The clothes and blankets were up on the terrace for drying under the sun. Shyamoli goes up to collect them. When she comes down the stairs, she finds a woman in a red-bordered sari waiting at the door with her eye on the eyehole.

'Who are you?'

Chintamoni turns to her and smiles, 'Don't you recognise me?'

Surprised, Shyamoli responds, 'Grandma! Where did you get this address?'

'Your sister gave it to me. Although I don't want to call her your sister. Your father has not married her mother. Open the door. It's very hot outside.'

As soon as Shyamoli opens the door, Chintamoni walks into the flat.

'Switch on the fan!' she orders, while taking off her sari. By the time she has finished the sentence, the old woman is already on the floor clad only in a blouse and petticoat.

Shyamoli grumbles, 'I don't like your attitude. The moment you are within closed doors, you take off your clothes.'

Shyamoli begins to fold the dry clothes she has brought down from the terrace.

Chintamoni complains, 'Stop pretending to be busy. This is not even your house. Go bring me a glass of water.'

Shyamoli retorts, 'So your son drove you away? I have told you repeatedly not to stay for more than two days!'

The old woman makes a face, 'Who told you that my son drove me away? It was that whore and her daughter. You go bring me some cold water.'

Shyamoli brings water in her own tumbler. The old woman pouts, 'Only water! The city has spoiled you. Bring some *monda* from the fridge.'

'There's nothing. No one has a sweet tooth in this family.'

The old woman mutters, 'Everyone is trying to lose weight, huh!' Shyamoli goes to the kitchen. Everything in this house is accounted for…*roti*, rice. Shyamoli is entitled to three *rotis* in the morning. For some reason, she has eaten only two-and-a-half and had kept half aside. She brings that on a plate along with some sugar. The old woman eats as if there's plenty of time at hand. She nibbles at the *roti* like an ant.

Shyamoli sits on the floor, 'What is your plan? Eat quickly and leave in ten minutes!'

'Your madam will definitely know me. I have been working in this neighbourhood for two years now. I am working for Shubho's mother for six months.'

'Madam doesn't know Shubho's mother.'

'Huh! I don't believe this. Shubho's mother knows her quite well. Married yet no kids. Everyone knows about your madam. People have also seen you with that driver's son.'

'Madam will not be pleased at seeing you.'

'Why? I have come to stay with my granddaughter for a night. Tomorrow morning, I will leave and set out to find work. Why will she object to that?'

'You have again taken leave from work without informing?'

'Ah! Why won't I inform? I had taken two days off, now ten days have passed. If they still want me, they will keep, else they will let me go. I will not beg them to let me stay. I will take you along, if you want; you may request them.' Chintamoni licks the sugar off her fingers.

'I won't go anywhere. Same drama every time! You will show this attitude and leave work and I will have to go and beg them.'

'If you don't want to go, don't bother. There is no dearth of offers for me. I will get myself a job.'

Chintamoni gulps down some more water and asks, 'Give me some catechu.'

'From where will I get catechu? If you want to apply lipstick...'

'Damn. If you lick it once, all goes away. Get me some *sindoor*.'

'There's none.'

'There are idols on the shelf. Your madam doesn't wear *sindoor*?'

'Madam uses lipstick.'

'Then just give me a mirror.' The old woman takes out a small flat *sindoor* box from inside her blouse. 'Bring me a comb.'

As Shyamoli brought a mirror, the old woman scrutinises herself minutely, 'It seems my lips have caught *sutika* and are bloodless.'

Making a path with the tip of the comb, she fills the parting of her hair with vermilion.

'Don't keep going to your son's place unannounced like that.'

'Why won't I? I am not afraid of that whore.'

'Your mouth is like a dirty sink. You have given birth to a sneaky mule. And now you keep blaming my mother.'

'Your mother, huh! You only take your mother's side! If only she had been your own mother!'

'There you go again…'

'You turn a blind eye. And there your father caressing that big fifteen-year-old girl! I've never seen him being affectionate towards his own daughter!'

This is where Chintamoni gets it all wrong. Despite being Rama's daughter, Shyamoli's face resembles Gana a bit. Fair complexion, wholesome physique and a chiselled face. Since the old woman had not been in touch with Gana for a long time, she has assumed Shyamoli to be the legitimate child from Gana's first marriage. It was only after four years of walking out of her marriage that Rama was able to bring her two daughters to her. Those years had been hell for Shyamoli. Every day, she had felt like a goat waiting for execution. Their drunk father was always ready to beat. Both the sisters would in turn get beaten up. Every day Kochi would ask on waking up, 'Whose turn is it, *didi*?'

'Your turn okay.'

'No. Look at the marks on my hand. Yesterday, he made them with his stick. Today's your turn.'

'Seems like it.'

'In that case, today I will have a full meal and you will fast. Remember you said the other day it is difficult to tolerate the beatings with a full stomach? Didn't you say that?'

'Fine. Today you eat. But tomorrow I'll eat and you'll fast.'

Their father would wake Shaymoli up in the middle of the night and say, 'Let's purify this house with some fire!' He would have a stick in his hand that had kerosene-soaked cloth at the tip. He would be completely drunk. God knows where he would get kerosene. He usually had matchsticks in his pocket, but he would forget this in his drunken state. Dragging her hair like a maniac, he would laugh and say, 'Give me some fire, immediately! I will burn all signs of your slutty mother.' Several nights, Shyamoli had to hide in the cowshed on the pretext of finding matchsticks.

The two sisters were thus quite happy in Rama's new family. Gana would often take them out and buy them clothes and bangles. But every few months, Chintamoni came over.

Now Chintamoni softened her tone, '*Natni,* please find me some work!'

'This is not your cup of tea. Go to the station and beg. You will at least get twenty-five rupees every day that you can give your son.'

'That is a lot of work. You will have to stay awake all day. Can't sleep in peace at night. People keep clawing at you, touching you in funny ways.'

Shyamoli gapes in surprise, 'You've begged too?'

'Only for six months. When that lame fellow brought me over the border from Faridpur and left me at Sealdah station… for six months I had to beg. Then one day I saw your father and followed him here.'

Now if one were to ask who the lame fellow was, the woman would start on her tales of romance. She has no shame.

She can tell you unabashed all the names of the people she has slept with in the last twenty years.

Shyamoli looks at the clock. 'Now go. Madam will return any minute.'

'Where will I go? What if the house I worked for does not let me in?'

'You will still have to go. You can't stay here. Go.'

Chintamoni replies in a dispassionate voice, 'Then give me four rupees to buy betel leaves.'

By the time Shyamoli brought the money, the old woman has already gotten dressed. She smirks while wearing the slippers, hoping Shyamoli will ask her the reason. But seeing her quiet, she whispers, 'I've heard a golden rumour. Your father has kept a mistress in the slum across the canal. Very soon your mother will be on the street with her daughter.'

Shyamoli shuts the door on her face.

After that day, Chintamoni did not come again. Shyamoli had waited for the first two weeks, thinking she would refuse to open the door to the old woman. But she was glad and relieved that the woman did not come. Her mouth was a reservoir for expletives. No one cared about Chintamoni. Sometimes when Rama called, Shyamoli would ask, 'Have you heard anything from Grandma? She has not come this way ever since I drove her away.'

Rama would scold, 'What's it to you?'

'What? I can't even ask if my grandmother is alive or dead?'

'You will be informed of her death, if it happens.'

After about twenty days, Shyamoli once again spots the filthy woman. On her way to buy cigarettes for the master of the house, she found her talking animatedly to Montu of the *paan* shop. God knows why the old woman flirted while talking to men, swaying her body like a *khyemta* dancer. Montu said aloud for Shyamoli to hear, 'O Rangeela look, it's your granddaughter!'

The old woman laughed and stopped Shyamoli, 'O *lateen*, where are you off to?'

Shyamoli said, 'Have you no shame! They are calling you dirty names! No trace of a husband yet you dress up like Rangeela in coloured clothes and go about like a new bride!'

The old woman grinned, 'You are also quite beautiful. But despite your age, you choose to dress like a widow. At your age, all my flowers had bloomed!'

Shyamoli said, 'Again you've started, you evil woman!'

The old woman responded, 'Don't get angry. I was going to ask you: will you go with me to a place tomorrow? It will only take a few hours.'

Montu sniggered, 'Will you take her to the park? Good. Go. You have already fashioned yourself as Rangeela. Now you can train your granddaughter.'

Chintamoni snapped, 'Why will I take her to the park? Will Prince Charming come for my granddaughter?'

Shyamoli started to walk away.

Chintamoni tried to catch up, 'So will you come along?'

'Where?'

'Beleghata. Will go check out the mistress your father has kept there.'

Shyamoli turned to her with a stern face, 'I don't want to see your face ever again.' She picked up speed.

Five days later, she gets a phone call from Rama. 'Can you come home for a bit, please?'

'What happened?' Shyamoli is anxious.

'It's been a week since your father has not come home. Kochi keeps crying; she has stopped eating.'

'Why do you keep crying for that worthless fellow? If he goes and starts another family, will we stop living?'

'Another family!' Rama repeats numbly.

Shyamoli urges, 'Now you've started too! Very good. Both of you cry and open a *kirtan* team.'

Rama chokes with tears, 'I don't know what to do. Your grandmother has come and puts up here. She has received news from Bardhaman that Gana's father has passed away. I broke her *sakha*, *pala* and helped her into a white sari. Now she has shut herself in a room. I have to coax her to eat, bathe…'

'Okay. I will come tomorrow morning.'

The train is delayed. Rama has to leave for work before Shyamoli's arrival. She has lain Babusona in the yard. The baby has started to cry in the heat. Kochi is nearby, mindlessly staring at the sky. This scene is not new to Shyamoli. She picks up Babusona in her arms and takes him to the shade. The baby stops crying.

Shyamoli tells Kochi, 'Get up, get some water for the baby.'

Kochi is still, staring blankly.

'What is wrong with you? Is your beloved dead?'

'Mind your language, *didi*!'

'It is because I have restrained myself that I have only asked you this. Otherwise you would have heard me saying, "Such a shameless girl! Just sitting idly like a heroine while mother works herself to death." For whom are you grieving? Is he your own father?'

Stomping away, Kochi leaves. Shyamoli makes Babusona drink water and then puts the baby to sleep. Opening the cover of the pot, she realises there is no cooked rice. All she can find is some pointed gourd floating in a sad curry in an aluminium bowl. Heating the oven, she puts water in a pot to boil, and washes rice and potato. She is about to boil water for tea, when Rama returns. 'When did you come? Did you have tea?' she asks.

'Who will make tea? Your darling daughter?'

'Oh, where is Kochi?'

'Wherever she is, she will come back once hungry. You go change. Then we will have tea. I have a headache.'

Pouring some oil on her head, Rama goes off to the pond. Once the rice is cooked, Shyamoli began washing last night's utensils. With the room empty, she can now cry. She cannot understand why she was crying. Who knew there was so much sorrow in her!

After she came back, Rama sat to eat in front of a plate of neatly arranged rice. Tears came to her eyes at the thought that it has been so long someone has looked after her.

'You haven't served your grandmother?'

'Is she here?'

'Yes, over there.'

Ever since she arrived, Shyamoli hasn't seen any trace of Chintamoni. On seeing the other room closed, she mutters, 'What new drama is this?'

Taking a morsel to her mouth, Rama says, 'This has been going on for three days now…'

Shyamoli knocks on the door with a plateful of rice, curry and boiled potatoes. She pushes the unlocked door and finds Chintamoni lying on a reed mat on the floor. Shyamoli fails to recognise her at first glance. Chintamoni seems to have visibly aged. The unkempt grey hair falling on the wheatish face makes her look like a ghost. Shyamoli hands her the plate without a word. The old woman starts on the rice, mashing it with her fingers. Giving her a glass of water, Shyamoli goes to finish her own meal along with her mother.

Rama askes while eating, 'Do you have any news of your father?'

'I don't have any father. Now will you also start crying, Ma? Then do something. First eat and then cry. You will be able to keep at it longer with a full stomach.' Rama quietly finishes her food. Shyamoli notices she ate more than she usually does. Perhaps, it was because on other days there's no one to make her eat with such care.

Rama begins to chew betel leaves. Noticing Shyamoli's surprised look, she says shyly, 'It's your grandmother's. It would have gotten spoilt otherwise.'

Shyamoli says, 'Lie down. Let me apply some talcum powder on your throat and neck.' Rama lies down like a child, undressing herself. After some time, she rests her head on Shyamoli's lap.

Shyamoli says, 'If you want to cry, cry. I will give you five minutes. Cry your heart out, then sleep.' Rama breaks down crying.

Shyamoli consoles her mother, 'We don't need men. You had to toil to feed yourself even when Gana was here, you have to do it now as well. Isn't it better to save your earnings and get Kochi married?'

'Honestly, you have no news of him?'

'You don't need to know. Let me sing to you.' Shyamoli sings, *Dorodiya Pakhi re shonar badhon, pakhi ti urailo ke...O golden chained Sympathy Bird, who made you fly away, who made you fly*. It is a song from Bangladesh. It has travelled from Saatkhira through CDs. Shyamoli has memorised it by hearing it playing in her neighbourhood programmes. Rama has fallen asleep. Shyamoli keeps singing all afternoon with her mother's head on her lap. This is the only song that came to her at that moment.

In the afternoon, she went out only to return in the evening with a shopping bag. 'Let's make *khichdi* today, Ma. With fried duck eggs and mango chutney.'

Surprised, Rama says, 'You've always hated *khichdi*. The two of you would keep fighting on this. One would want *khichdi*, the other boiled rice.'

'You take a rest today. Your younger daughter is sitting near the pond and muttering things to herself. The smell of *khichdi* should be good enough to drag her home.'

Rama sits down to cook. There's a plastic packet in Shyamoli's left hand. Rama hesitates to ask what is in it. If she chooses not to say, there's no point coaxing her. God knows how she will react with a string of harsh words. Before Rama finishes cooking, Kochi returns. Seeing her, Shyamoli enters the room and shuts the door. At night, both sisters eat heartily, cleaning the pot. Chintamoni is served only *khichdi*. She finishes her food and goes to bed, leaving the plate unwashed.

When Rama wakes up in the morning to start the oven, she is surprised to find Shyamoli is already up.

'Why did you wake up so early? You could get some more sleep…'

'How many saris do you have, Ma?'

Rama smiles softly, 'I have a nice silk one. Do you want it?'

'No. It will be best if it is a traditional sari, but it has to be colourful.'

'There's a trunk underneath the bed. Take what you like.'

Shyamoli selected a yellow cotton sari with a red border. 'Can I take this? You won't get it back.'

'Why do you suddenly want to wear a sari?'

Shyamoli smiles. This gives Rama the courage to egg on, 'Will have to get you married.'

'First, let's arrange one for Kochi. It is difficult keeping unmarried daughters at home in these areas.'

'She is so lazy. I don't know how she will be able to manage a household.'

'If the situation arises, she will have to do it. And we are not getting her married immediately. Start looking for a groom; let's begin by saving some money.'

'If the groom's family asks for the father, what will we say?'

'Tell them, the father has abandoned us and started a new family.'

Shyamoli entered Chintamoni's room to say, 'Freshen up and get dressed.'

Chintamoni stares blankly, 'Where will you take me?'

'Kolkata. Who will take your responsibility here? Your son has left, there's nothing for you here. You won't be able to digest the food bought by that whore's money.'

'Is this the way to talk about your mother?'

'Why don't you go to your son's new family in the slum across the canal?'

'Did he ever do anything for me? It is your mother who will do everything.'

'Oh now you've realised that! Come let's look for work. You'll visit again after two months. Even if your son's not here, that whore will surely take care of you. Now, get up! We have a long way to go.'

In the train, Shyamoli bought almost everything that came their way—puffed rice, *ghugni*, groundnuts, ice sticks, cucumbers. But nothing could make the old woman eat. Shyamoli did not pester her to. The old woman looked like she would start crying anytime. They reached Sealdah without any fuss. Much to Shyamoli's relief, Chintamoni was unusually quiet.

On reaching the station, Shyamoli handed her a two-rupee coin.

'What will I do with this? Bus fare is six rupees.'

'With this, you go to the ladies toilet.' Shyamoli gave her the red bordered sari. Then she took out yesterday's packet from her bag.

'Take this. There's *sakha*, *pala*, sindoor. Put a round *bindi*, wear these bangles. Then have a *paan* and redden your lips. I am waiting outside here.'

Chintamoni is dumbfounded, 'My husband is no more. How can I wear these?'

'Did your husband ever feed you? You have to work to get food. So it is better to keep yourself happy. You are Rangeela. You will remain so. Don't get stuck in these rituals.'

The old woman stared wide-eyed for some time, then broke into a laugh. 'I wish I could dye my hair.'

'There's no time. First let's find you work. Then there will be time for all that.'

Sari in hand, Chintamoni went off dangling the packet. The old woman is incorrigible. Her old gait, a particular flirtatious style of swaying her ass, is back. Shyamoli opens her bag desperately looking for a handkerchief. While crying, it is usually her nose that leaked more water than her eyes.

Translated from Bangla by Saheli Biswas

Bandhni

Sunanda Bhattacharya

Kalu

The dog continued to sit with its head turned towards the sky; its eerie moaning cut across the wind, now for three days on…time and again. Its howl was a complaint to both God and Allah. Umaben's head began a rapid tattoo. She knew the crying of a dog was an omen for bad things, but how much worse could things possibly be? For the last three days, an earthquake had unsettled Umaben's entire spirit, shaken her flesh and bones. She knew it was impossible to escape the pain of that. She got up to open the box of *rotis.* A small stale piece of *bhakri* was left. She took it in her palm, crossed the *otla* and pushed the heavy wooden door to reach the street. She advanced towards Kalu, the dog who sat right in the centre of the street. All around, the road was strewn with stones and bricks, shards of glass, iron rods, bicycle chains. On the left, slightly far away, Fakirbhai's *bandhej* shop still spouted a thin thread of smoke. By the footpath, three wooden carts had overturned their wares: apples, bananas, radish, tomatoes and cucumbers were lying scattered on the street. Tabrez's cart, from which he sold *besan* fritters, was upturned too: a group of flies hummed over a stash of rotting onions and chillies coated with flour. All around, burnt and putrefying smells made their way upwards. The smell of dried blood mingled with them and created invisible ropeways to hell. Umaben felt nausea grip her throat at the overpowering odour. Her three-day empty stomach churned in revulsion. She had stepped out of her home after three long days. Slowly, she tiptoed through the debris strewn on the road, picking her way with care. Kalu was sitting at the crossing. Umaben called out as she waved the *bhakri* at him. Kalu looked at her and turned away. Umaben moved forward and said: '*Roti, jomle baap.*' Eat the bread. But the dog showed no interest. She noticed some pieces of bread strewn about the road; some others must have tried to dissuade the creature from howling. Umaben looked at the dog: its head on the ground, Kalu lay supine, ignoring her. A sigh escaped her throat: *Ha Bhagwan*! Oh my God!

On her left, a small group of people talked in a murmur. A few policemen stood nearby, looking at her. One of them waved his hand, gesturing at her to leave. Kalu began crying again. Umaben's heart leapt up in fear. Day before yesterday, the men had poured petrol over Fakirbhai and had burnt him alive. There was not a soul in the neighbourhood who had dared to intervene. Fakirbhai used to tell her, 'Ben, even God is afraid of the poor and the naked.' He was fearless about his poverty, but he did not know that someone who was feared by God could become a target for Satan.

Umaben turned away from the crossing and walked like a robot to the small shop that was once owned by Fakirbhai. It had no signboard now. She pushed open the door to the small room. Kalu came running and stopped in front of the open door. It then turned back once again to go back to its old place. Umaben went in with slow steps; the floor was covered in rush mats. On it lay a piece of white silk cloth. Numerous threads were tied on it and on the other side were marks of a design made with pencil. Nearby stood three big aluminum pans filled with blackish water. Umaben suddenly had the sensation of someone standing at her back. She turned and saw that a policeman had entered the room.

He asked, 'What are you doing here?' In a soft whisper, she said, 'Nothing.' The policeman ordered her to return home. The situation was grave. It was dangerous to walk about. One didn't know when the arms-totting cow-eating *miyans* would descend on the neighbourhood. The situation was *nazuk,* very grave.

The Situation Was Grave

Umaben had never imagined that such things could happen. All her beliefs lay shattered. She had seen many of the men who were part of the mob grow up from adolescence to maturity. How could they? Come in a horde, pull someone out of his home and stab him, all in the name of God? The mob had some women too; they were suitably encouraging the looters and killers. The Muslims, too, had voted for councillor Meeraben Chabria. The same Meeraben who had visited every home in the neighbourhood with folded hands to say, 'Please give me a chance to serve you.'

Who knew that to serve was to evict? Jubeida Khatun had not known that and neither did the others who had voted for Meeraben. Meeraben did not know it herself that within a few months after she got elected she would see herself in that role. Meeraben had understood that the journey from councillor to member of the legislative assembly (MLA), from MLA to a minister was tough and that she had to show her prowess. There was too much internal competition within her party; she had to prove herself. At that instant, the incident had happened. A train was set on fire! Everyone had raged with anger: What arrogance! Killing and targeting Hindus! The very next day, after a secret meeting, the decision had been made—to loot Muslim shops and businesses, set fire to their houses, raze to the ground what they owned. The attacks had taken place with war-like precision: the houses had been marked earlier so it was easy to target them. Those who could escape, did, others died at the hands of the mob. Women were raped, old men beaten or set on fire. When the mob left, the air had been thick and sticky like pus. As night deepened, the police came to the same houses and started a combing operation. They picked up young, able-bodied men and took them to jail. They had information that the young Muslims were planning to retaliate so it was better to put them under lock and key. Those had been the orders from above. The situation was grave, so preventive measures had to be taken.

Benpani

After lunch, Umaben surreptitiously descended the stairs and crossed the small lane to make her way to the *madarsa*. Instead of taking the main road, she followed the smaller lanes to reach the back gate of the school. The sturdy wooden gate was locked and she knocked quietly on the thick panels. After a while, a small aperture opened and a young man peered out. In a rough voice, he asked her what she wanted. In a soothing tone, Uma said, 'I have come to see Jubeidaben.' An older man who had perhaps followed the young man now peered out. Abdullabhai recognised Umaben. He asked the young man to open the door and when Uma entered, Abdulla took her up two flights of stairs. The school was packed with women and children, filled to capacity but everywhere there was a strange hush. Even the smaller children were not running about. A few babies sometimes cried out, but were immediately quietened down. What were the mothers telling the children to keep them still and silent? 'Someone will burn you alive…' Maybe that was the sentence mothers spoke to them. Umaben felt shooting pains in her legs. Had they gone numb?

Abdullabhai showed her the room where Jafar's family had taken shelter. When Jubeida saw Uma, her familiar welcoming smile was absent. Her daughter, Mehrunnissa, was to get married that day. She was sitting huddled in one corner of the room. Jubeida's young son, Kausar, was crying in a nagging way, '*Amma bhuk laigu.*' Jubeida scolded him to keep quiet; there was nothing to eat, she said. Umaben could not find words to speak. Jubeida was her *benpani*, her best friend for many years. Even if they had met four times in a day, their conversations never dried up. Umaben suddenly wanted to talk of those happier days, but she stopped herself. It would be so terribly out of place. It would seem like mockery to speak a few words of reassurance. The thought came to her that may be she could take Kausar home with her, but then she stopped herself. Her family, her neighbours would not tolerate it. Hadn't she heard enough times that old adage: Don't trust a Muslim. They would not allow her to trust a seven-year-old boy. One never knew: they could snatch him away, pour petrol and... Uma's eyes hazed over. Jubeida's face looked smudged, her features indistinct. The police had arrested Jafarbhai and his elder son, Ashraf. Ashraf was only twenty-two. Jubeida had no idea of their whereabouts. Her blood ran cold as fear clutched her heart. At that moment, the arrival of her best friend created not a ripple in her mind.

A few young men had come to peer through the room's doorway. Abdullabhai came back to ask Uma to leave. She got up to go on legs that seemed lifeless. Jubeida sat with expressionless eyes, without uttering a word, just like a living corpse. Uma wanted to hear her say, like old times, 'Sit down, you have just arrived.' Where was her old friend, that talkative Jubeida, her *benpani*?

Uma and Jubeida were old friends. Their friendship had begun when they were both in primary school. They lived near each other and went to the same school. They had been inseparable; even outside school they had always been together. Jubeida belonged to an affluent family, while Uma's mother had a tough time bringing up her two girls, Uma and Krishna. When the cotton fields were harvested at the end of winter, the mother would collect small tufts of cotton from the buds and sell them. The two girls would often join her in the fields. Sometimes, Jubeida, too, came along to help. One day, Uma had forgotten to shut the box where their mother stored *rotis* and ants had got inside. Her mother had slapped her for being careless. As tears rolled down Uma's cheeks, Krishna had angrily cursed the ants, '*Musalman nu chhe.*' Red ants belonged to Muslims because they bit, black ants to Hindus because they did not. The children had heard these words of wisdom from a young age. Uma remembered scolding her sister, '*Chhi*! Don't speak such nonsense!' Jubeida had come soon after. She had asked, 'What is the matter?'

'Nothing!'

'Tell me.'

Krishna said, 'Ma has slapped Didi.' When Jubeida had heard the cause, she wanted to run home to get *chapatis* for her friend. But she did not. She knew Uma's family would not eat them. The injunction was too strong to break down. She had looked helplessly at Uma, eyes full of love. They had acted as a balm to Uma's pain. In the midst of all her poverty and hurt, the flower of friendship had bloomed perfect.

When the girls were in class nine, Jubeida was married off. The two friends had wept together at the thought of their parting. After a few years, Uma, too, got married and went to the same city where Jubeida lived, Kazinagar. And wonder of wonders, the two friends came to live in the same neighbourhood. Kazinagar was famous for its *bandhni* cloth, patterned in intricate designs created by tying threads. Jubeida's husband, Jafarbhai, had his own business selling that; he ran a huge shop. Uma's husband, Harishbhai, worked in a rice store. Kazinagar was much bigger than their old Viramgam town. Nobody had time to keep tabs on their neighbours. The friendship of Jubeida and Uma blossomed once more in the anonymity of a big city. Uma could come to Jubeida's house to drink tea or eat *faluda* ice cream. However, when Jubeida cooked meat, Uma felt nauseous at the smell. So during her visits, Jubeida was careful never to cook it. Uma's in-laws were a bit peculiar. Harish's family was made up of five brothers and they all lived in the ancestral house. Each family had a room and a kitchen, and everyone lived separately. No one bothered with any one else. In the beginning, Uma had felt strange. What kind of a family was that? How could brothers live so detached and separated from each other? However, she soon got used to it. Her husband had a steady job and although he didn't earn much, they had managed. Uma had known poverty since childhood, so an ease of living had seemed like an achievement to her. After Hitesh's birth, they had been happy. But her happiness had not lasted long. When her son was eleven, her husband died suddenly. Uma was all at sea. How was she to raise a child? On those days of struggle, Jubeida had come to her rescue. She had taken her *benpani* to Fakirbhai, so that she could learn the art of making *bandhni* cloth and make a living for herself.

We Will Take Care

Jaffarbhai's shop was the largest and busiest in the city selling *bandhej* goods of all kinds. Saris, *salwar kameez*, *pagdi*, fabric—a huge stock starting from three hundred rupees to many thousands. The shop was always full of customers who came from nearby villages and cities. The small decorations on *bandhni* saris of all hues—red, green, yellow, blue—sparkled with an inner glow.

That huge business had attracted the ire of certain people. How long could such a business be allowed to run? As soon as the opportunity arose, they looted the shop. At first, the looters and arsonists took the expensive goods, and in the next wave, the less costlier ones. Then they set fire to the shop—only Jaffar's shop was burnt. The next shop, Ambaji Bandhej Bhandar, had remained intact. Umaben knew many of the looters. She had recognised them as she stood on the terrace watching helplessly. As soon as she had come down, Hitesh had asked her what she had been doing for so long on the terrace. He knew his mother had seen the handiwork of his friends. Hitesh also knew that his mother visited the *madarsa* regularly.

He had asked her, 'I believe you go to the *madarsa* every day?'

'Yes, I take milk for Kausar.'

'Don't go anymore. I warn you!'

The police had arrested Jaffarbhai and Ashraf and there were no news of them. Umaben had wanted to be near Jubeida, but Hitesh, whom she had borne, was no longer recognisable. Her limbs ached with a strange tiredness. Uma longed to see Hitesh be more like Ramanujbhai.

That day, all the Muslims of the locality had been herded together to safety. They took shelter in the house of Ramanuj Pillai and his wife, Sudhaben. At night, Ramanujbhai had heard of an impending attack on his home. Worried sick, he had called up some people and procured two Jeeps. He had put saffron flags on the bonnet and had taken the terrified men, women and children to Afzal *madarsa*. Ramanuj Pillai was a Hindu, but he had not hesitated to save Muslim lives. The arsonists had declared war on him. 'We will take care of him later,' they had said. Pillai was from Kerala but he grew up in Gujarat. His ancestors had lived in Kazinagar for three generations. Ramanuj's wife Sudha belonged to Gujarat, yet they were considered outsiders. Ramanuj was a blot on the face of Hinduism; he was an enemy of other Hindus. He needed to be taught a lesson but it was better to wait for a while. There were too many media reports all over the country, it was better to lie low. Hordes of reporters had descended on the city. They were investigating cases of arson, rape and murders, aided by some people in the city. They would have to be taken care too.

Umaben

Everybody had been shifted from Afzal *madarsa*. Most of them went to Panigate camp. Umaben wanted to find out where Jubeida had gone, so she went to ask Ramanuj Pillai. He assured her of help. Sudha brought her a steaming cup of tea and sat near her, drinking her own. Uma's heart bloomed at that simple human gesture. Her son wanted to throw her out and her other relatives too avoided her. She remembered her last conversation with Hitesh.

'All Muslims are disloyal. They are Pakistani stooges.'

'How did you know? Have you forgotten all that Jubeida aunty had done for us?'

'One or two Muslims may be an exception but all others are traitors.'

'You have learnt to kill, loot and set fire to innocent people's homes.'

Umaben's voice had chocked with unshed tears. Hitesh was annoyed to see his mother's weakness. After Umaben began learning *bandhej* art from Fakirbhai, Hitesh had noticed the bond between them. Sometimes, while returning from school he had to pick up the house keys from Fakirbhai's small shop. He had often noticed his mother's radiant face as the two conversed together. At twenty-one, Hitesh had understood that empathy was detrimental to an ambitious life. If one had to earn a livelihood, one had to toughen one's mind and heart. It did not do to be too soft. Hitesh's mentor was Navkishorebhai, who was a *swayamsevak*. He had given Hitesh a good idea. Navkishore controlled all the rice mills of the area. He had whispered in Hitesh's ear that if Muslim rice mill owners were removed, Hitesh could easily get to control one. But for that, he had to take part in the battle. Hitesh had no qualms about that. He was, therefore, annoyed with his mother who did not understand that ultimately Hitesh would profit from the riots. He had no qualms about threatening his mother. 'Stop going out to search for all the Muslim neighbours who had to flee their homes. Stop searching for Jubeida aunty. Stop showing empathy for traitors.'

Empathy

Empathy was a terrible thing; it weakened oneself. It did not allow one to fight and win wars. Lord Krishna had urged on the battlefield, 'Arjun, get ready to fight your near and dear ones,. Those who could get rid of their empathy would be the ultimate victors. Hitesh had threatened to throw Uma out of the house. On the other hand, Jubeida had implored, 'Don't come here anymore. You are endangering yourself.'

Uma had asked, 'You don't want me to come and see you?'

'Try to understand reality. You and I are now separate… different.'

How would Jubeida explain to Uma that it was better to avoid each other; that it would be the best possible way? With Uma's visits, Jubeida's family got marked and the possibility of attacks increased so much more. Especially as Hitesh was part of the arsonists' gang.

After thirty-eight days of imprisonment, Jaffarbhai and Ashraf had returned. Jubeida was relieved to see them unharmed, without a scratch on their bodies. She did not want to jeopardise their safety by earning Hitesh's ire. Uma did not understand all that. She felt Jubeida rejected her because she was a Hindu. She felt a deep sense of hurt. How could she apologise to Jubeida? Could she apologise on behalf of all Hindus? Did Jubeida not know that Hindus like Ramanuj Pillai existed too? Uma felt a great sense of rejection. Her heart wanted to say, 'Jubeida, my *benpani*, don't forsake me.' But, of course, Uma did not say a word. She got up to leave. Jubeida had seen her going, eyes misty with tears. When Mehrunnissa called her mother for lunch, Jubeida did not eat a morsel. In all the past weeks of trouble, she had not shed a single tear, but Uma's pain-filled eyes made the fire inside her go out. Jubeida began to weep in earnest.

Hitesh was busy. Every day he had to finish his job at the rice mill and then work with Navkishorebhai. The

Special Investigation Team (SIT) was arriving the week after. Navkishorebhai was busy discouraging people from testifying in front of the team. For some days now, Hitesh was looking for an opportunity to have a talk with him. That evening, he broached the subject of getting his hands on Rajkotia's shop. Navkishore simply said, 'I will see.' Hitesh knew there were others in the line ahead of him who were wealthier than him. He knew he had to do something big to show his worth to Navkishorebhai.

But just then a terrible thing happened. Among the people who came to testify in front of SIT was no other than his own mother. Umaben said that she had seen the people who had set Fakirbhai's shop on fire; people like Praful, Anant and ten or twelve other people. There was not an inch left in the community hall where the hearing was taking place. Hitesh had turned to stone as he heard his mother's testimony.

That night, Umaben could not enter her home. Hitesh had locked her out. Sudha Pillai had to give her shelter, but a few days later Uma had come to live in Fakirbhai's burnt-out shop. Kalu the dog came running.

A few days later, Umaben went to air force colony to look for some orders for *bandhni* cloth from the officers' wives. She also managed to get a few rupees as advance payment. She bought some fabric. She needed to start work: to create *bandhej* full of colour and sparkle. Some days, she would turn to Kalu, her companion, and ask, '*Su Kalu, Fakirbhai ni yaad aweche*?' Do you remember Fakirbhai?

March had come again, the month of Falgun. It was that time of the year when the Flames of the Forest blossomed with orange flowers. In Committeebagh, there were four or five such trees. Every day, Uma carried a basket to collect them and keep them for the whole year. The orange that was extracted from the flowers was brilliant in hue. Fakirbhai Rangrez, the master craftsman, had taught her to make colours from different flowers and trees: Flame of the Forest, the bark of the *arjun*, tamarind and *babool* trees, the colours of the *parijat* flower and pomegranate skin, and the blue *aparajita*, the unvanquished. Fakirbhai had taught her all the secrets, like making resplendent green by mixing the correct proportions of blue and yellow.

Uma collected the flowers that had fallen from the stems and went to rest on a small earthen mound. The spring sunshine caressed her shoulders softly. She felt almost intoxicated. That sunshine perhaps came from another world where people laughed and loved, sang and talked to each other with love. Umaben hummed a song softly under her breadth: *Ek ewa ghar moley, ya kasa karan bina pon jai soku...* The song hid all the sorrows of a homeless life, the wish to enter a home where one could go without any reason. Homeless Jubeida still lived at Panigate camp. Umaben felt a weightlessness assail her through a composite sense of freedom because she was homeless too. It was good Hitesh had made her so.

She stood up with her basket of flowers. She thought she should go and see Jubeida once. But then she changed her mind: she ought to use the orange flowers to make a *chunni* for Mehrunnissa whose wedding was just a few days away. Uma would imprison the colour of autumn sunshine through the magic of her fingers. And it was late. Kalu was waiting for her. Uma felt compassion stroke its gentle fangs on her breasts. Empathy had strong twines; she was imprisoned in its web.

Translated from Bangla by Debjani Sengupta

Sun and a White Bird

Joya Mitra

It was already dusk, but there was no sign of them. Sreelata was getting a little anxious. It was dark and in the autumn months of Kartik, the air was cool. Bolli's tonsils were bad and she suffered all through the year with cough and cold. If she caught a cold...

On top of it all, their neighbour's daughter, Anwesha, had gone along. Of course, Anwesha's mother, Chitra, had suggested it: 'Let them go together, Mashi will be pleased.' Mashi was Subala who worked in both their neighbouring homes as a maid. She worked in three other houses, but not on the same street. She arrived at seven in the morning, first to Sreelata's, to work like a machine, then left for Chitra's house. Chitra started her household activities early; her husband worked in a factory and left at seven. Subala finished work at Sreelata's home and then went to Chitra's to help with the cooking and washing. Cooking the rice, chopping vegetables, all such chores! After Subala finished her work in the other houses, she came back to Sreelata's in the late afternoon to wash the dishes and make *rotis* for dinner. Only then was she free to go home herself.

Subala had been working for many years at Sreelata's home. The year Purbo went up to the fifth standard, his nanny went off to get married and Sreelata had decided against keeping a full-timer. Subala had come that year. Purbo passed his Higher Secondary exams, went to college and now ran a small printing press with his computers.

Subala had remained, coming twice to their home, working all these years. Purbo never completed his studies. In his second year in college, he left, saying, 'Why must everyone have a college degree? It's a superstition.' When Sreelata had got angry, he had laughed and said, 'Ma, tell me why graduation is important? For a job? Can't you see thousands of graduate and post-graduates roaming around without occupations? Look at all my friends, desperate for a good position after their studies. Now I don't think of getting a job, I will do my own thing. I will give businesses to others in the future, trust me...'

'If you don't have a degree then people will think you are uneducated,' Sreelata had argued.

'Never mind people, Ma. I love reading. How many students read like I do?'

Sreelata remembered a few years ago Purbo had asked her if he could read books meant for adults. Sreelata had answered that there were no such books, only good books and bad. And now, that same boy read about things that Sreelata had never heard about: Purbo had told her about the helix that was the DNA, about new discoveries in the cosmos, Carl Sagan's theories, so much more! When did he read all that? Sreelata suddenly remembered one evening as she was sitting down to write an article on the November Revolution when she had raised her eyes to see her mother standing at the doorway. She had said with joyous surprise, 'When did you come? Why didn't you call me…?'

'No, I was watching you. How small you were, hidden within my stomach, a small girl who had learnt the alphabets sitting in my kitchen, and now you know so many things that I do not...'

Did all mothers have that same sense of wonder?

Purbo had also said, 'Remember, Ma, how you had once said that the education given at schools and colleges made no sense; it did not equip any one to deal with the world.'

Yes, Sreelata had said that once. She had also believed that. She had burnt her degree, had left University, but some of those who had been a part of that youthful rebellion were now professors in many colleges. How did that happen? While they were destroying their certificates, did their leaders surreptitiously finish their university courses? Sometimes, Sreelata felt a swift shaft of anger, but she had no regrets about her own life. How many people had the right or the inclination to think with independence? That was surely something of an achievement in a life. Therefore, they had not forced Purbo to follow the beaten track. Everyone had a right to choose their lives and as parents they could guide their children till a certain age, but it was impossible to force a child to follow the impositions of parents. Purbo had asked Sreelata the last pertinent question: 'Ma, will you be ashamed of a child who is not a graduate?'

No, she would not be ashamed. It was necessary to give up feelings of shame for new things, things one was unaccustomed to. He was not like us, so he was no good, he was an ugly duckling—all such strictures were swept away in time. When she was incarcerated in jail, was her mother ashamed of Sreelata? She did not know. Was there a place to feel shame after the terribly sharp anxiety and horror? And all the other mothers whose children had been like her? If they had felt shame, then would they have gone to the police stations day after day to cajole and argue with the policemen? Would they have crowded the gates of government jails to meet their 'convict' children? Or shared information with strangers who had suffered the same gut-wrenching pain of having a child in jail? Sreelata's sister, Preetilata, had recognised Kaludada's mother as she was wearing a sari she had recognised as belonging to her jailed sister. At the Behrampur jail entrance, Swati's father had recognised Basudev's father and had taken him home. No, it was not shame, but in spite of the fear and the pain, there was a hidden pride that had kept all these men and women tied to each other. After twenty-six days of police torture, when Dalia's mother had been given permission to meet her, the first question that she had asked her daughter was: 'I hope you never spilled any names to the police'. Potu's mother had asked the same question: 'You didn't tell them the names of anyone else, I hope?'

Sreelata might feel sad, she might argue, she might be angry, but she would not feel shame that her son was breaking the codes of society. But at times like these she often felt that she had given too much freedom to them, that it would end in disaster. She had warned them to come before dark. Where were they? The darkness was deepening. And there was Anwesha. It was not a small distance that Subala travelled to and fro. Times were frightening.

When she heard Purbo and Bolli's voices at the front door, Sreelata kept her face stern. They, however, did not notice. In excited voices, they recounted how happy Subala was to see them, how much fun they had had with everyone, so many other experiences. Bolli was even more voluble than Purbo: 'Ma, the huts are so pretty! The earthen floor, the earthen courtyard decorated with white chalk drawings. The straw thatched huts had creepers over them with white flowers were so lovely!'

Purbo laughed at his sister: 'Oh, you have only seen them from afar. If you had to live in those huts, then you'd know. The rooms had a musty *gobar* smell, you know, Ma.' But he

happy to see that small figure: at least one bird had escaped the silly cruel fingers of that man.

Sreelata had been unwell so Krishna and Jonaki had been permitted to stay with her at nights. They ate the roasted Bengal gram and the *mots* slowly, little by little, over many days. Only the little duck was kept aside, brightening up the prison cell. Krishna had been arrested from Jadugoda along with members of Ananta Singha's group. She and Mary were lodged in Hazaribagh jail. In the last two years, in the three cells of Presidency jail, they had talked of those days and of Mary a number of times. Mary Tyler was British who had worked in Germany as an interpreter. She had fallen in love with a Bengali engineer, Amalendu. In the seventies, when Amalendu came back to India to join the Naxal movement, Mary, too, came with him. In the jungles of Jadugoda, she had shared all the hardships of the group. When she was arrested, she had escaped the brutal police torture meted out to others because of her nationality, but her embassy had pressured her to return home. Mary had refused. She had reiterated that she had a valid passport and visa to stay, and there were no proven charges against her. She had never thought of asking for any special privileges because of her race and when Krishna had been shifted to Presidency, Mary had continued to give support to all the village women who had been prisoners in Hazaribagh jail with her and to stand by them. After four long years, the police had got together the charge sheet and created the Fourth Tribunal to start trials. The people incarcerated in Hazaribagh would be brought to Kolkata, so Sreelata and her companions were expecting Mary to arrive any day.

The three decided that they would not eat the yellow duck. It would be kept aside for Mary. How else could they welcome a beloved companion in the jail cell? In the long boredom and ennui of a prisoner's life, only another of them would understand the significance of that gift of the figurine.

Two weeks went by, the Fourth Tribunal sat for two days. The news of Mary's arrival got lost in the banal routine of their lives. Krishna had to appear in court, but even she did not know anything. Summer was on, the jail meals comprised okra and rice or *bajra rotis*. The cooking was worth emulating. The vegetables were boiled with salt and turmeric in big iron woks. They were neither cleaned nor washed. Then a few red chillies tempered in oil were poured over the boiled mass. In large iron drums, the vegetables and rice arrived in the wards for distribution. The okra was perhaps especially bought for the inmates; they were so long and so fibrous that people said the boys in Presidency jail dried them and burnt them to make tea. The jail doctor had made provisions for Sreelata and her companions to drink some tea every day, but most days they were neither given sugar nor milk. In 1972, the public distribution of ration outside the jail was very stringent; each adult was given a minimal quantity that was not enough to feed even a child. Except for the ward-keepers, all the female inmates of the jail had a perpetual hungry look: they seemed more like starving beggars than political prisoners. Sreelata and her companions were no exception, but their combined willpower enabled them to protest when lactating mothers were given insufficient food, laugh away hunger pangs or threaten the jail authority with a strike. It saved them from despair but all-around things were bad.

It was easy to fight direct tyranny or opposition; they kept themselves wakeful to garner their protests. It was the excitement of being alive. When the iron shackles tightened, they realised they were living through fear and hatred to those in power. But time inside the jail was like a dead river: without currents, without movement, boring. Every day was like the day before. Incarcerated, they kept time with the arrival of meals: morning brought black gram boiled with pieces of clay and stones, afternoon meant blackish okra and black-coloured *dal* and one spoon of rice, evening brought blackish dal, black-coloured okra and two dirty *rotis*. Week after week, it was the same. It was difficult to ascertain if the week comprised ten days or two years, the day had thirty-six hours or five. Those days, inside their melancholy unquiet cells covered with dirt and grime, filled with musty unwashed clothes and quilt, on one corner lived the yellow duck standing atop an upturned steel bowl platform, nestling over a printed blouse.

Dragging its chained feet, the month of April went by. On the last day of the month, the friends sat up at night, thinking of ways to celebrate the next day, their favourite. All over the world, free men and women would be celebrating with songs, flags and banners. What would they do to be a part of them? The three of them, out of which one was lying on the quilt on the floor, vomiting blood?

Sreelata had fallen ill. Gathering all her strength to stay alive, to find the power to sing a few songs, she had become even more sick. Jonaki sat next to her pillow, trying to clean the red-coloured vomit with her paralysed right hand. Krishna and Jonaki had been like a mother, no, more than a mother, who had stood battling Death, cradling their sick friend through the night with love. They had culled many poems from memory to recite it to her. At dawn, Sreelata had dozed off. Probably so had the two friends, their four human arms wrapped around her. Sreelata did not know if they had slept at all or if they remained awake all through the night. In the morning when she awoke, she saw Krishna and Jonaki sitting there with a tea-filled glass and a steel plate decorated with newspaper chains. It was to celebrate May Day. They had propped Sreelata against the wall to see the arrangements of their festivity. In the midst of the torn paper chains and next to the tea, were two tiny web-feet, coloured red, two small sugar pieces of the yellow duck.

'Why didn't you save them for Mary?'

'We don't have feet, but that doesn't mean we are imprisoned. The duck has given us her feet to celebrate.'

'Think of the duck as swimming freely for when ducks are in the water you don't see their feet, do you?'

The three friends had broken into giggles.

Did that duck come back after so many years, bleached white by Time, swimming through a river of love?

'What are you doing sitting there alone?' Sreelata heard her husband call. She got up from the chair and stooped to take the sugar duck in her palm. As she went past Purbo's room, she saw the children huddled together, reading something on the computer screen. Sometimes, the fire raged, sometimes it remained hidden under the ash, but it was indestructible. Fire was the warmth of the sun buried in the unnamed soil. How could it ever get lost?

Translated from Bangla
by Debjani Sengupta

Writing

Kalyani Thakur

Gouranga Gachhi's youngest daughter has just finished her graduation with Honours in Bangla from Bogula College. She is trying for a job, taking entrance exams. She has also collected the form from the primary school. The exam will be soon. Many of her classmates are also sitting for the exam, all in a group. At last, when the result is out, it is established that Rekha Gachhi's name is on the panel. She clears the viva too. They ask about her father's occupation. She says it is cultivation. She has also talked of her family's condition. She does not know the words in English to describe how her father climbs palm trees to collect its juice, so in a hurry she had said, 'Cultivation.'

She will start work at Kalagachhi Primary School. Meanwhile, she has completed all formalities, like going to the DI office, etc. Her father knows how to count to twenty. He has not been to school. At home, a one-eyed blind grandmother lives with them. Her clothes are not too clean, she is unable to walk properly. All day long, she sits in a corner to soften betel leaves in a bamboo pounder and chews *paan*. If someone comes near, she speaks a few words in short sentences. While going from one thatched hut to another, she bends double.

When she saw her own name in the panel, Rekha came to pay her respects to Thakuma, her grandmother. Today is the first day of her school. Yesterday, Thakuma had asked her how many children studied in her school. Rekha has seen about a hundred. Next to the school is a Muslim neighbourhood and some others come from the *Jeley* fishermen caste, *Bagdi* and *Namashudra* children, too, and a few children from Ghosh families. Thakuma had asked her to buy a hundred pens. Rekha did not have the time to ask why she wanted pens.

Before leaving, Rekha goes to touch Thakuma's feet. Quietly, the old woman asks: '*Kolomgula nichis*? Have you taken the pens?'

'No.'

'You did not ask why I wanted them.'

'Why?'

'Give one to each child. For thousands of years, our people have not known how to write. Even when they had eyes, they were blind. What other people wrote had been the truth for them. Give the pens to all the students, my child, so that they can write to mask a thousand years of those writings. Tell them that. Now go, you will be late.'

The girl returns from school. At dusk, she sits under a hurricane lamp to study. After some time, she dozes off in tiredness. Meanwhile, the nib of the pen clutched in her hand starts to fly. Up and up it goes till it resembles a gigantic snake that covers the sky to start a storm and then a rainfall. It begins to fall as ink, black ink. On Earth, all the pages of the religious texts from the temples, mosques and churches are swept out by the storm. Everywhere in the cosmos, those pages receive the black-ink rainfall and are cleansed of their words. The girl starts running over those sopping pages, bewildered. Wherever her limbs touch a page, it comes out white and the children who have followed her footsteps, sit down on those pristine pages and begin to write a new history.

Translated from Bangla by Debjani Sengupta

Draupadi Has Woken Up

Renu Behl

Shadows of the silent night had begun to lengthen. But there was still some commotion in the tin-roof shacks selling the local brew on the outskirts of the village. Nihal Singh had reached along with Charan Singh as soon as the sun had set. Charan Singh was his childhood friend and knew well enough what troubled him. He knew that his own home seemed alien to Nihal Singh since Bebe[1] had passed away and he had become weary of his own life. As the two drank, Charan Singh tried to draw Nihal Singh back towards life. Nihal Singh kept listening to his friend. As he steadily grew more intoxicated, Nihal Singh became quieter. As they were leaving the shack, Charan Singh tried to persuade his friend to come along with him. With stumbling steps and faltering tongues, sometimes in raised and sometimes in lowered tones, leaving some things said and some unsaid, sometimes to each other and sometimes to themselves—the two began to walk back towards the village.

They came to a fork where their ways parted. The village lanes were deserted at this time of the night. The sound of frogs croaking somewhere in the distance broke the silence. A stumbling foot hit a dog sleeping beside the path; who woke up with a squeal, stepped back then seeing the man walking on began to bark at his retreating back. He stopped and turned. With an ugly expletive flung towards the dog,

1 Form of address for mother in Punjabi. This story, while written in Urdu, is based in rural Punjab and much of its idiom and local flavour is from the Punjab.

he resumed walking. The door of his house was locked. He banged the door loudly two or three times till Pammo opened it. She went towards the kitchen mumbling something under her breath. He went and sat down on the *takht* laid out in the courtyard. His Bebe used to always sit on this *takht* when she finished all her errands. He spread his hand lovingly on the cloth covering the *takht* and began to wipe his wet eyes with his sleeve. Pammo returned within a couple of minutes carrying *dal* and roti for him. Without a word, she put the food down beside him on the *takht* and turned to leave when he held her wrist and asked: 'Has Makhni gone to sleep?'

He called his younger brother, Makhan Singh, Makhni as a form of endearment.

With a wrench Pammo freed her wrist and began to walk back towards the kitchen without uttering a word.

'I won't give you any more trouble; I'll go away.' And he began to eat the food. He was completely full with the alcohol. He barely ate two morsels, left the rest of the food and took the stairs going up to the roof. Like always, his bed was laid out under the open sky. He fell down upon it. When he looked up at the star-studded sky he could see Bebe's face among the clouds. When he tried to open his eyes again, the strength to do so had left him. Lost to the world, he fell into a deep stupor.

Nihal Singh was not an alcoholic. Normally, he drank just about five or six times a year—when there was an especial sorrow or a happy occasion such as a wedding. Though, yes, every three or four months, if he made a plan to go to the whore in the city he would glug down some liquor on the quiet. But he never had the effrontery to drink in the village and appear before Bebe. He was the only one in the entire family who was scared of falling foul of Bebe; or, let us say, he didn't want to do anything that would cause her pain. His younger brothers Makhan Singh and Baisakha Singh drank all the time and Roda Singh was way beyond Bebe's control; he had become an addict long ago. Like thousands of other young men, he too was addicted to opium and cannabis. He was beyond fear or regard.

Nihal Singh lay like the dead all night. When the sun shone bright overhead Makhan came to wake his brother. There was a time when Nihal was used to waking up at the crack of dawn. Every morning Bebe's sweet voice would be heard, reciting the Gurbani; it was always this sound that he woke to. He always found the mornings to be sweet; he realised this only after Bebe passed away. Now the mornings seemed insipid, the days colourless, and the house looked deserted. Little did he know then that the life and soul of that large household was none other than Bebe. Sitting on the *takht* in the courtyard, Bebe's eyes would take in every inch of the house. Her voice was so strong and vigorous that Pammo could barely squeak in front of her. In fact, he had barely ever heard Pammo's real voice properly. He had never felt the need to speak to her. At one command from Bebe, Pammo would fetch whatever he needed to eat or drink. Her head covered, Pammo would go about quietly working in the house, never uttering a word. On several occasions Nihal Singh had tried to address Pammo via Bebe, and Pammo too would look at him from the corners of her eyes; oat such times, Nihal Singh would sense that Pammo was smiling. Once, in Pammo's hearing, when he praised the food she had made to Bebe, she was clearly listening to everything. When Bebe added two words of praise, Pammo stood smiling. Nihal had asked Bebe, 'Has an injustice been done to Makhan?'

'Why?'

'What if she is mute?'

'Go away! She can hear and speak. Ask Makhan...how much gossip she tells him.'

'It's hard to tell, Bebe,' he had said softly.

She kept listening to every word without saying anything as she went about her chores.

Changing the topic, Bebe said, 'I am thinking of speaking to Chanan.'

'Why?'

'I'll ask for his daughter's hand for you?'

'Do you know her age? She's at least fifteen years younger to me. Her father will never agree to the match. Don't keep your hopes up.'

'Hai! Hai! There's a famine as far as girls are concerned.'

'Why do you worry, Bebe? I am not the only bachelor in the city. If not here, my wife will be somewhere else. If she's written in my fate, I'll find her. After all, our Makhni found his Pammo.'

'I can't sit and do nothing. I know exactly how her father agreed to this marriage. I had gone with your proposal but they liked our fair and handsome Makhan.'

'So what, Bebe? I am her *jeth*. And in the twelve months of the year, there is one month of *jeth*,' he said, smiling naughtily, as he looked towards Pammo who was washing clothes at the time. Bebe swatted him lightly on the head and said, 'She's your younger brother's wife; don't tease her.'

***

Time passed. Bebe's efforts yielded no fruit. Truly, there was a famine as far as girls were concerned. After all, Bebe too was

not have imagined in her wildest dreams that she would find it so difficult to get a bride for her favourite son. Every time she returned home empty-handed after the hunt for the elusive bride, she would say: 'It seems there is a famine of girls. Everywhere you look there are only boys. And if perchance you find a girl, then family has such airs...they seem to want nothing short of a big landlord!'

Bebe's worries increased as time passed. Four grown up boys and that too without a father, they had no one to fear or respect. They went about the village like bulls on the rampage. To pass time, they would drink and play cards, or hang around near the village pond and leer at the girls and women passing by, or else pass comments on the films they had watched on their mobile phones. Bebe was anxious to tie them down with the chains of domesticity and responsibility. She could not safeguard their youth from spilling over. All the time, she was fearful that they might stray and do something so shameful that it would forever cast a cloud over their lives. Every now and then, she would caution them. She would address her old mother-in-law and say: 'Are you happy now with four grandsons? Do you call this a home? No one has any fixed time for coming or going, nor do they know how to conduct themselves in polite society. If they had had a sister, they would not have roamed around naked like this all around the house. There is not a single woman in the entire village who is ready to visit us in our house because of these wretched fellows and their ways. Now, I have begun to feel that any one of them should get married. Things might improve if even one girl comes to live here. This house looks like a den of ogres!'

The old granny lived a long life and passed away without seeing any of her grandsons dressed as a groom. The four brothers managed the fields among themselves. Bebe looked after the house and the cattle. By now, she was tired of all the chores. Moreover, she was worried: how would their line continue? The other day her friend Manjit was telling her how the Chaudhry's son had run away with a village lad. What if one of her sons were to do the same? The very thought made her tremble with fear. She could no longer sit and do nothing. Once again, she launched upon a crusade of finding a bride. This time, she met with success. She had gone with a match for Nihal but Pammo's parents preferred Makhan. Despite all her misgivings, she had to eventually give in and agree to marry Pammo with Makhan. Things improved somewhat since the arrival of the new bride.

Nihal, in fact, had found it a bit odd seeing the new bride roaming around the house. He was the eldest son, and had he got married he would no doubt have wanted to immerse himself in the tinkle of bangles and the muted song of anklets. But now he had begun to keep himself away from all this. He tried to spend as much time as he could outside the house. Before Pammo's arrival, he used to sleep in the courtyard with his brothers during the summers. Now the brothers slept on the roof. There used to be all three of them up on the roof; now there were only two because Roda had begun to spend all his time outside the house. Despite all their efforts, Bebe and Nihal could not free Roda from the clutches of drugs. Soon, he stopped coming to the fields despite all their persistence and began to demand his share of the land. Everyone knew why he wanted his share. His great-grandfather had 50 acres which had dwindled over the years to 10 acres by the time his father had inherited it. Now these 10 acres were to be divided into four portions.

Bebe tried to placate and scold him by turns but when Roda remained adamant, Bebe asked for a fifth share: that was her share. Roda took two acres and left the house.

***

Soon, Pammo took over most of the household chores. Bebe would sit in the courtyard and help as she read from the Holy Book. But she would also be mindful of Nihal and Baisakha's needs. By repeating it time and time again, she dinned it into Pammo's head, 'Look here, till your elder and younger brother-in-law get married, you are the one who has to do all their chores. You have to be mindful of all their needs. When their wives come, it will be another matter, but till then you must not step back from your duties.'

And Pammo would nod her head ever so slightly and say 'Yes'.

One night, Nihal and Baisakha ate their meal and went up to sleep on the rooftop. They talked for a long time till finally, Baiskha said somewhat hesitantly, 'Brother, I have to say something important to you.'

'Why were you talking about unimportant things till now?' Nihal turned around and asked.

'I was wondering if I should say it or not.'

'What can it be...out with it! I am sleepy...tell me quickly: what is it?'

'Jagtar is taking his truck to Calcutta on Wednesday; he's asked me to come along. I am thinking of going with him.'

'Why do you want to go with him?'

'I...' He began to stutter.

'Look here, Baisakha tell me everything clearly. I know Kartar and I have an inkling about your inclinations. Tell me, what is it?'

'I am tired of all the talk among our people. Lads much younger than me make snide comments. Men I grew up with, shared my childhood with, now cross the path when they see me, and if I were to go to the home of any one of them, they send me away from the door itself. Just because I am not married, it doesn't mean that I have no respect.'

'Where does the question of "respect" arise in all this? Bebe tried so hard to find a girl for us... What can anyone do if we are not destined to get married? Moreover, we are not the only unmarried men in the village...there are so many others like us.'

'I don't have your patience.'

'What do you mean? Why don't you speak up clearly?'

'I will go to Calcutta with Jagtar and find myself a wife there. He says it is easy to get a girl there.'

'I see...so you will buy a wife!'

'If that's what you want to call it.'

'Bebe will never agree to it. She will never accept a Bengali as her daughter-in-law. And think...you will have children tomorrow... Sikh children looking like Bengalis!' The very thought made him laugh out loud.

'Whatever will happen will be for the best. They will be my children, after all,' Baisakha retorted.

'Look here, Baisakhe, it's your life and you can live it whichever way you like but I know that Bebe will never agree to this. She got enraged when she heard about the barber's daughter, Kamlesho...so what if it was the widowed daughter of a barber, she was from our neighbourhood! Who will understand what she says if you bring home a Bengali?'

'I don't care...it'll be good if she doesn't understand others and no one can understand her. At least I will have a family of my own. At least people will stop talking.'

'Think once again. Talk to Bebe, get her to agree before you go off with Jagtar.'

'That's the difficult part. I'll try to talk to her... But, brother, why don't you speak to her on my behalf?'

'If I ever have anything to tell her, I will; why should I speak to her for you?'

'Aren't you my elder brother?'

'All right, go to sleep now; I'll see what can be done in the morning.'

And it happened exactly as he had feared. Bebe was furious. She refused to agree to Baisakha's plan. When Nihal tried to intercede, she began to cry. Tears and that too in Bebe's eyes! Nihal gave up and Baisakha stomped out of the house in anger. That night he didn't return home. Nihal went looking for him at Jagtar's place. Somehow or the other, pleading and cajoling, he brought his brother home but Baisakha did not abandon his plan. On Wednesday morning, he took a bag and left the house. Bebe wept and wailed but he did not stop. For three months there was no news from him. Then, one day, he suddenly appeared with a Bengali bride in tow. He fell down at Bebe's feet.

'She's your daughter-in-law, Bebe. Give her your blessings.'

She looked at the weak, thin girl with the huge black eyes in the dark-skinned face that beseeched her helplessly for mercy. One look at her and Bebe clutched her head and said instinctively, 'What have you brought?'

'She's your daughter-in-law, Bebe. I have married her.'

'How much did you buy her for?'

'I didn't buy her, Bebe. She's the daughter of a poor father. I simply helped—not just her father but my father-in-law.'

'It's called buying. And a woman who has been sold has no respect—not in the house nor in the society at large. People will not respect her and nor will you in the days ahead.'

'She's my wife, Bebe. Don't say that. I have to live my life with her. Please, just give us your blessings.'

'Listen to me: you did as you wanted to. You did not listen to us. You are responsible for your own decisions. Take her with you and set up your own household. There is no place for you in this house.'

'But where will I take her and go?'

'You should have thought of this sooner. You have many well wishers; surely, they will give you advice.'

By now, the news had spread in the entire village. Nihal too heard it and came running towards his house. He saw people craning to peer into his home and became enraged: 'Is there a drama happening here? Go, go away, scoot!

Hearing his booming voice, the crowd scattered.

'Bebe, what are you doing? Why are you creating a spectacle? He has married her; not run away with her.' And, keeping a hand affectionately on Bebe's shoulder, he began to speak to her.

'But see what this wretched fellow has done!' And tears began to rain down afresh from Bebe's eyes.

'Stop crying, Bebe. It's happened. Now calm yourself.' And he clasped her to his chest and began to quieten her down.

Baisakha stood transfixed with his bride, looking worried. Pammo was working in the kitchen and peering out.

'Go on, Baisakheya, take your wife inside. Go wash your hands and eat something.'

Baisakha heard this and drew a breath of relief and beckoning to his wife to follow him, quickly went indoors.

'Pammo, go and see if they need anything,' he hardly ever addressed Pammo by her name.

He saw Pammo enter the room Baisakha had gone into with his wife and resumed placating Bebe. He didn't quite like the way Baisakha had married a Bengali girl and brought her home. He could fully empathise with his pain, deprivation, desires, needs, and his longing. After all, he was riding in the same boat. The only difference was that he didn't want to do anything that would cause pain to Bebe. He too wanted someone to look out for him, to wait for him, to speak sweetly to him when he returned bone tired from the fields. He too longed for the sound of children's voices in his home. But he simply sighed and stayed quiet.

Soon, the remaining eight acres were further divided. Baisakha took his share of two acres and crossed the threshold to set up his own home with his new wife.

People have seen the divisions of homes and properties. But here Bebe's heart was divided. Her hopes and dreams dissolved with her sighs and tears out of sight of everyone's eyes. She had no bodily affliction; only her soul was in torment. The love for her sons ate away at her like termites that eat up a piece of wood from inside and leave it hollow. The sense of failure at not being able to have her most obedient and loving eldest son married tormented her till one day she left the world with her most ardent wish unfulfilled.

Pammo and Makhan did their best to look after Nihal after Bebe passed away. Makhan would work in the fields with him. They would go together to the *mandi* to sell their grain. Makhan would try his best to ensure Nihal did not stop on the way with his friends. Pammo too tried her best to look after all his needs: ensuring he got his meals on time, washing his clothes, laying out his bed on the roof—she would do all this without being told. Still, the house no longer seemed like his own home now to Nihal. He had begun to call it Pammo's home. The veil that used to cover her head had slipped now that Bebe was no longer there. Perhaps Bebe had taken with her the feeling of ownership of the house. Roda had long since sold his share of the land and gone away who knows where. Baisakha was happy with his Bengali wife in his own home. Only Nihal was left, all alone. He remembered Charan Singh's words. The very words that he had refuted the first time were sounding good to him now. He began to wonder how long he could live this meaningless life. How long would he keep going to the whore, and feeling like a thief, just to fulfil his needs? He too needed someone of his own. Baisakha was happy. People talk for a day, two days and then fall silent. What if one has sallow or dark-skinned kids? After all, they will be his own. How he had laughed when Baisakha had said the same thing to him. He was tired now.

At night, the two brothers sat on the *takht* eating their meal and Pammo was getting fresh, hot *rotis* from the kitchen. Nihal casually mentioned Charan Singh.

'Makhan, that Charan Singh is putting a lot of pressure on me to go along with him.'

'What?'

'He's been telling me to go out with him for a few days.'

'Out? Where?'

'He has some relatives...they know a lot of people. Maybe I'll find a girl I like.'

'Really, brother!' And he looked at him with amazement.

'What can I do? After all, I too have my needs, my desires. I can't live alone anymore. The soil of Punjab has become barren for me.' He spoke in a tone laced with despair.

Glossary

Bangla

Bandhni/Bandhej (Hindi): a technique of tie-and-dye colouring of fabrics, especially common in Gujarat and Rajasthan

Bauri and Bagdi: low-caste Hindus in the caste hierarchy of Bengal, generally doing agricultural work in other high-caste landholders' plots

Belauz: blouse

Bishohori/Manasa: goddess who ruled over snakes. She is worshipped among tribal people and lower castes to save them from snakebites and smallpox

Chunni (Hindi): a long cloth used both as a scarf and to cover the head

Ghugni: chickpea curry eaten as a snack

Tushu: a female deity worshipped to prevent seasonal illnesses. The worship of the goddess is prevalent among the marginalised peasant communities in Bengal

Kaka: Uncle, father's younger brother

Kala bou: dark wife, said in jest or affection

Khas land: government-owned land

Khyemta: an indigenous dance form, mainly by women

Kirtan: community singing of songs mainly of Vaishnavite origin

Khichri: a meal of rice and lentils cooked together, eaten on its own or with side dishes like eggs, fish or vegetable fritters

Jalebi: sweets made with flour and sugar in circular shapes with variations of patterns and whorls

Machan: a platform built of bamboo and straw

Mashi: aunt/aunty, a kinship term often applied to strangers or older women

Mahajon: landlord or trader

Monda: sweetmeats

Miyan: a term used for Muslims, sometimes in a derogatory way

Otla (Gujrati): courtyard

Paan: betel leaves

Swayamsevak (Hindi): a member of the Hindu right-wing organisation—Rashtriya Swayamsevak Sangh (RSS)

Shivrattir: the day of worship of Lord Shiva accompanied with fasting

Sindoor: vermilion

Shakri: after eating or cooking, the right hand is considered impure and has to be washed before it can touch clothes or utensils

Shakha/pala: the white and red bangles that Hindu married women wear in Bengal

Sutika: anaemia

Thakuma: paternal grandmother

Lateen: a variation of natin/natni, or granddaughter

Urdu

Abba: form of address for father

Amma: form of address for mother

Arhar: a sort of pulse

Babu: form of address for a young boy

Bhaiya: form of address for brother

Bhabhi: form of address for sister-in-law (brother's wife)

Bindi: a dot on the forehead to signify a woman's married status

Bua: a form of address for an older woman or a maid servant

Dulhan/Dulhan Begum: while 'dulhan' literally means bride, it is also used as form of address for the daughter-in-law of the house

Hafiz: usually used for one who has memorised the Holy Quran but often used for any learned man or one well versed in religious matters

Jeth: name of a month (the third month of the Nanakshahi calendar, approximately equivalent to May–June) and it also means elder brother-in-law

Mamu: form of address for mother's brother

Maulvi sahib: who knows or teaches the Holy Quran

Pukka: when used for houses or roads meant to signify permanent or cement-based in contrast to *kutcha* which is unpaved or uncemented and uses mud or earth

About the Editors, Contributors and Translators

Editors

Debjani Sengupta is the author of *The Partition of Bengal: Fragile Borders and New Identities* (2015) and has edited *Mapmaking: Partition Stories from Two Bengals* (2011). She has co-edited with Rakhshanda Jalil and Tarun Saint an anthology called *Looking Back: The Partition of India 70 Years On* (2017). Her translations from Bangla have been published in *Essential Tagore* and the *Oxford Anthology of Bengali Literature*, volume 2. Among her other translations are writings by Selina Hossain, Tasleema Nasreen and Tilottama Majumdar. She teaches at Indraprastha College for Women, Delhi.

Rakhshanda Jalil is a Delhi-based writer, translator and literary historian. She has published over 25 books and written over 50 academic papers. Her recent works include *Liking Progress, Loving Change: A Literary History of the Progressive Writers Movement in Urdu* (2014); a biography of Urdu feminist writer Dr Rashid Jahan *A Rebel and her Cause* (2014); an edited volume of critical writings on Ismat called *An Uncivil Woman* (2017); a literary biography of the Urdu poet Shahryar (2018); *The Great War: Indian Writings on the First World War* (2018); *Kaifiyat*, a translation of Kaifi Azmi's poems (2019) and *Jallianwala Bagh: Literary Responses in Prose & Poetry* (2019). She runs an organisation called *Hindustani Awaaz*, devoted to the popularisation of Hindi–Urdu literature and culture.

Contributors

Anita Agnihotri has served in the Indian Administrative Service. Among her significant novels are *Mahanadi*, *Akalbodhon* and *Jara Bhalobeshe Chilo*. Her work *Mahuldihar Din* has been translated as *Forest Interludes: A Collection of Journals and Fiction*. Her poetry has been collected in *Anita Agnihotri Kobita Shomogro*.

Aniqa Naz was born in Karachi in 1969. She received a PhD in organic chemistry from the University of Karachi in 2002. Aniqa started her literary pursuits with Urdu ghazal writing during her student years; she subsequently moved on to Urdu short stories. Her first story, *Irtiqa*, was published in a local Urdu literary magazine in 2003. A number of her stories were published later. She died tragically young in a car accident in 2012.

Azra Abbas was born in 1948 in Karachi. She earned her master's degree in Urdu from the University of Karachi and went on to teach Urdu literature at a government college in the city. Eventually, she and her husband, the poet and novelist Anwar Sen Rai, moved to England, where she currently resides. In 1981, her first work was published, comprising a long feminist prose poem in the stream-of-consciousness technique entitled, *Neend ki Musafatein*. She has produced five collections of poems and one of short stories, along with an autobiographical narrative called *Mera Bachpan*.

Fahmida Riaz was Pakistan's foremost feminist writer, activist and poet. Her poetry collections include *Patthar ki Zaban*, *Badan Dareeda*, *Dhoop*, *Kya Tum Poora Chand Na Dekh*

Paaoge, *Hamrakab* and *Aadmi ki Zindagi*. She was proud of her work as a translator, from Sindhi and Persian, especially *Khana e Aab-o Gil*, the first translation of the *masnavi* of Mevlana Jalaluddin Rumi from Persian into Urdu. She published several collections of short stories and novels, such as *Godavari*, set in India and *Zinda Bahar Lane*, based in Bangladesh. She was given the Himmett-Hellman Award for Resistance Literature by Human Rights Watch, New York, in 1997 and the Sitara-e-Imtiaz by her country in 2010.

Jhumur Pandey lives and works in Silchar, Assam. Her two acclaimed collections of short stories are *Jol Khaben Bonodurga* and *Sukh Gacher Golpo*. Her poems can be seen in *Kichu Bolar Chilo*. Her stories for children have been collected in *Pisti O Sei Swapnopakhi Surela*.

Joya Mitra is a writer and activist based in Asansol, West Bengal. Her autobiographical work, *Na Hanyaman,* has been translated as *Killing Days: Prison Memoirs*. Her latest book of poems is called *Kalo Mayur Nacho* and her non-fiction is collected in *Joler Naam Bhalobasha* and *Robbarer Panchali*.

Kalyani Thakur is a Dalit feminist writer and poet who had been writing since childhood. Her recent collection of prose pieces is called *Phire Elo Ulongyo Hoye* and her autobiography is titled *Ami Keno Charal Likhi*. Her poetry has been collected in *Chandalinir Kobita*. She is associated with the Dalit Sahitya Sanstha.

Kishwar Naheed was born in 1940. She moved from her home in Bulundshahr, in western Uttar Pradesh to Lahore in 1949. Her first poetry collection, *Lab-e Goya*, published in

1968, marked her as a bold new voice and a welcome addition to the country's fledgling feminist movement. Her poem *Hum Gunahgaar Auratein* became an anthem of protest during the worst excesses of General Zia's dictatorship and has remained an enduring symbol of resistance in the decades since. Each successive collection of poetry has bolstered her reputation as a fearless crusader for human rights and progressive thinking.

Maitri Roy Moulik is a geologist and has been educated at Presidency College, Calcutta, and Rutgers University, USA. Her profession and love for travel have provided her the material for her writing. Maitri's short stories have appeared in leading magazines in Bangla and her first novel is titled *Grohonkaal*.

Manju Bala was born in 1948, months after her family was displaced by the Partition and settled in West Bengal. She is an active member of Dalit Sahitya Sanstha. Her collection of poems is titled *Ashwarohir Apekkhay* and her prose pieces have been collected in *Chaturtho Bishwer Chitralekha*.

Papree Rahman is a well-known writer from Bangladesh whose collections of stories are *Mridu Manusher Motion Picture* and *Mamuli Jibaner Joltorongo*. Her novels include *Pora Nodir Swapnopuran*, *Boyon* and *Palatia*. She has a master's degree from Dhaka University.

Renu Behl was born in 1958. With masters' in Public Admin, Political Science and Urdu and a PhD in Urdu, she has written several collections of Urdu short stories like *Aaeena*, *Ankhon se Dil Tak*, *Koi Charasaz Hota*, *Khushboo Mere Aangan ki*, *Badli Mei Chhupa Chand*, *Khamosh Sadaye* and *Dastak*. Her

Urdu novels include *Gard Mei Atey Chehre* and *Mere Hone Mei Kya Burai Hai*, a novel on transgenders, and a Hindi novel titled *Kasturi*. Apart from award on books from various Urdu Academies, she has received the Shiromani Urdu Sahityakar Award from the Punjab Government in 2014 and the Award of Excellence conferred by the Chandigarh Sahitya Academy in 2015.

Sadiqa Nawab Sahar is a bilingual poet and fiction writer. Her short stories and novels depict the small but sensitive social realities of our times. Her works include *Kahani Koi Sunao: Mitasha*, *Jis Din Se*, *Khalish Benaam Si*, *Mannat*, *Pattharon ka Shahr* and *Angaron ke Phool*, among others. She teaches Hindi at KMC College in Raigad, Maharashtra.

Sara Shagufta was born in 1954 in Gujranwala in Pakistan. Sara upset every conceivable notion of literary and social propriety in the rarefied world of letters in Urdu and Punjabi. The major concerns in her poetry are her disillusionment with her married life, the separation from her children and unsatisfied passions. She went through clinical depression for most of her life and after two unsuccessful attempts finally committed suicide at the age of twenty-nine by throwing herself before a train in Karachi. Her poetry is found in her collections published posthumously as *Aankhein* and *Neend ka Rang*. Her close friend, the Punjabi writer Amrita Pritam, wrote two books based on her life: *Ek Thi Sara* and *Life and Poetry of Sara Shagufta*.

Selina Hossain is an acclaimed writer from Bangladesh, who has authored several works among which novels like *Purno Chobir Mognota* and *Japita Jiban* have received critical attention.

She has been awarded the Ekushey Padak in 2009 and has authored a number of short story collections.

Sujata Roy was born and brought up in Sainthia, Birbhum, West Bengal, and has a master's degree in Bangla. Her book of poetry is called *Diyotima* and her prose pieces have been collected in *Ami Boro Hoye Gelam*. She is a businesswoman.

Sunanda Bhattacharya was born and educated in Tripura but has lived and worked as a teacher in various parts of India. Her critically-acclaimed short story collections are *Borderer Golpo* and *Chanchtolay Rode*. Her latest novel is titled *Jhapsha Bihan*. She lives in Delhi.

Zahida Zaidi was a woman of many parts: a Professor of English at Aligarh Muslim University, a well-regarded Urdu poet, dramatist, actor, literary critic, a radical feminist and a lifelong voice of the liberal Left. Her long years in Aligarh did not, in any way, make her either provincial or cloistered; if anything, she was a citizen of the world. All along, her concerns were wide-ranging and catholic, and her voice that of the free-thinking, non-conforming, free radical. Her novel *Inquilab Ka Ek Din* is partly autobiographical.

Zakia Mashhadi belonged to an urban, educated, middle-class family with roots in western Uttar Pradesh, India. She completed her BA and MA in psychology from Lucknow University in 1966. An avid reader, she started her writing career in 1974 and has since published five collections of short stories in Urdu and translated more than a dozen books for prestigious literary organisations like Sahitya Akademi, National Book Trust and Khuda Bakhsh Oriental Public

Library, Patna, from English and Hindi to Urdu and vice versa. She has also written more than a dozen booklets for rural neo-literates in simple Hindi and Urdu. A new collection of short stories titled *Ankhan Dekhi* and a novelette, *Parsa Bibi ka Baghar*, are due shortly.

Zehra Nigah was born in Hyderabad, India, and migrated to Pakistan with her family in 1947. She began to recite her poetry at *mushairas* from a fairly young age, which was considered unusual at the time. Treading the fine line between feminism and feminine poetry, she has steadfastly refused to allow gender to dictate her choice of subjects in a poetic career spanning six decades. A popular voice and presence in the male-dominated *mushaira* circuit, she has held her own through the sheer grace and substance of her poetry. She has published three collections of poetry: *Shaam ka Pehla Tara*, *Warq*, and *Firaq*.

Translators

Daisy Rockwell is a painter, writer and translator living in the United States. She has a PhD in South Asian literature and has translated numerous works of fiction from Hindi and Urdu, including Upendranath Ashk's *Falling Walls*, Bhisham Sahni's *Tamas*, Khadija Mastur's *The Women's Courtyard* and Krishna Sobti's *A Gujarat Here, a Gujarat There*. Her political paintings have been exhibited internationally. Her work can be found at www.daisyrockwell.com.

Lipika and Rajorshi Das: Lipika Das was born in Barisal, now in Bangladesh, and lives in Kolkata. Her family had been uprooted and divided by the Partition. Her son, Rajorshi—a queer, non-binary poet—is a Doctoral candidate at Iowa University, USA. He teaches at the Department of English, Indraprastha College for Women, Delhi.

Saheli Biswas has completed her MPhil from Jawaharlal Nehru University, New Delhi, and is currently preparing for her Doctoral work on Indian Dalit Aesthetics. She worked as an Assistant Professor at the Department of English, Indraprastha College for Women, Delhi. Currently, she teaches in West Bengal.

Shahruk Rahman is a writer and translator from Bangladesh. She has translated Sahidullah Kaiser's celebrated novel *Sangshaptak*. Her translations of contemporary feminist writers of Bangladesh like Selina Hossain and Rizia Rahman have been published in anthologies like *Fugitive Colours* and *Caged in Paradise*.